Surprised By God

SURPRISED BY GOD

by ROBERT K. HUDNUT

What It Means to Be a Minister
in Middle-Class America Today

ASSOCIATION PRESS   NEW YORK

Publisher's stock number: 1659

Library of Congress catalog card number: 67-21144

 72

Printed in the United States of America

To my parents

Foreword

Robert Hudnut has written a most interesting and perceptive account of his first years as a pastor of a local church. It took some courage for so young a minister to make this record available. I am very glad to commend it because it shows how many-sided the ministry can be.

Mr. Hudnut does not fit into any of the ministerial stereotypes. He combines political activism with the most careful attention to the personal problems of people. He is still struggling to find intellectually satisfying expressions of his faith. He avoids the one-sided interpretations of the Church that today are prevalent and is convincing in his emphasis upon worship, teaching, pastoral help for those in the fellowship, and mission in relation to the world.

This is an account of the work of a very able young minister who is still in a formative stage. Many who read this book who are also in the early stages of their ministry may be inspired to find more opportunities in the pastorate than they have yet discovered. Others who read it will be both encouraged and fascinated by this picture of the many-sidedness of the profession.

JOHN C. BENNETT
President, Union Theological Seminary

New York, New York

Preface

This book offers the reflections of a minister on his job. They can scarcely be dignified by calling them a "journal." They are closer to a running commentary. For one reason or another, an event made an impression and was recorded.

This means, of course, that the notes which follow are highly subjective. They are one man's reaction. However, the events that happened, except for running for office, are, I venture to say, quite typical. The birth and death and hell of one parish are probably not too different from that of another.

I have not published these notes to "sell" anyone on the ministry. Nor have I published them to frighten anyone away. I have published them only to give a feeling for what a minister is and why I, a father of three in suburban Minneapolis, happen to be one.

I did not become a minister because I had "found God." I became a minister in order to find Him. And, on various occasions over the last few years, I have been surprised by what I have found—or, if you want to be "orthodox," by what has found me. Grace is serendipity.

Special thanks are due the Rockefeller Brothers Theological Fellowships for getting me to a seminary, the faculty and students of Union Theological Seminary in New York City

9

for keeping me there, and the six hundred hardy souls of St. Luke Presbyterian Church who endure my ministry among them with a faith, hope, and charity that surely rank them among the saints.

ROBERT K. HUDNUT

Contents

1. Pastor   13

2. Preacher   33

3. Politician   49

4. Priest   71

5. Teacher   87

6. Planner   99

7. Person   111

1

Pastor

Bear one another's burdens and
so fulfil the law of Christ.

Galatians 6:2

Our whole conversation today was like
a prayer, wasn't it?

Paul Tournier
Swiss psychiatrist

Today I saw diabolism in all its starkness. A man wants to desert his wife. Or, as we say in our modern patois, he wants to divorce her. They have been married a number of years. There are children. We are the only ones who know it. Just the three of us. It is more than I can bear alone. That is why I write it down here, I guess. It is more than they can bear alone, too. They have to tell it to other people. Telling it to me isn't enough. Nor is "telling it to God." We've got to get other people in on this. People who have walked the way before. Who in my congregation will be willing to listen to this couple? What other couple will be willing to tell their story, too? I am afraid to ask anyone. And because I don't, something is missing. Something at the very heart of the church is missing.

An unwed mother's mother comes to me. A boy and a girl who share an apartment come. A man who wants to leave his wife. A boy shooting dope. Who am *I?* Why do they come to *me?* They come for God. I am forced to try to release God for these people. They back me to the wall of my study. I feel like exploding through it to God. But God is not there. If people only knew that God is not there for pastors, too. We're all in it together. There is a cross on the wall over my left shoulder. God wasn't there for Him either. The temptations. The end. "My God, my God, why hast thou forsaken me?" The only way is to bring that cross off the wall for these people. How do I do it? My God, my God, how do I do it?

15

Sometimes it is hard to go on. Your people hurt you too much. You try to bring healing and they refuse it. You go months with a couple and they give up the struggle. A boy runs away, and the parents won't talk. A young man on parole holds up a grocery store. It affects your sermon writing and your praying. It affects your home life and your sleep. You have trouble concentrating, eating, and talking. The only way out, if there is one, is to have a small group of people who will share the hurt with you. If that isn't the church, then I don't know what the church is.

I walked across the graveyard tonight. It is on the way home. We laid the woman's husband here a few weeks ago. Death is the great mystery, of course. We took a poll in a church I used to serve to see what sermon people wanted to hear most. Immortality won hands down. We never know, that's the mystery of it. We never know, and we're mad to find out. I wonder now what this old man discovered. Tell me, old man. But there is only the cold and the dark and the snow. All I know is that this was a good man we buried here. And his goodness was with me as I walked across the graveyard tonight.

It is dangerous the way I become a good actor. After hundreds of prayers at hospital bedsides I know my lines pretty well. This does not mean that I am unable to communicate. Actors get through to the audience. That is their job. The danger is that the patient is not communicating with me. I do not let him. I say my lines across his bed and exit. Nothing of him goes with me. I have not dared let it. I hurt enough without his hurt, too.

Actually, the opposite danger is more real. I empathize too much. Occasionally I even think I have the patient's symptoms. Doctors get over this sort of thing in medical school. They know it impairs their effectiveness. But ministers are not always able to. And there is some question whether they should. Empathy may enhance rather than impair *their* effectiveness. A brusque doctor is one thing. He is treating the body. But a brusque minister is a contradiction. He is ministering to something more than the body. He is suffering with the patient. Suffering love is all the Christian has.

One of our officers died suddenly. That afternoon we had a special service of memory for him. That night I called a little girl to wish her "Happy Birthday." What is extraordinary about this job is that it keeps you in touch with birth and death, love and hate, joy and sorrow. When a baby is born, you are there. When a man dies, you are there. When a man and a woman want to live the rest of their lives together, they come to you. When they are fed up, they come back to you. This means that a minister must be flexible. He must be able to go from death to birth in a matter of hours, or from a divorce to a marriage in the swing of his door. I'm afraid I'm not always as flexible as I should be. And as I said "Happy Birthday" to the little girl, I hope she did not hear the sadness in my voice for the death of my friend.

There is a real danger in being with people so much of losing myself. It is the old preaching danger all over again. I am available day and night. I spend literally hours sometimes with individuals. I go wherever and whenever there is trouble. In a sense, my life is determined by other people's lives. This would be fine if there weren't so many people in *me*—and if there weren't four more people at my house whom I haven't begun to know yet. The only way out is to block time each day for self, others, family. Only an emergency should be allowed to interfere with the block.

A college student dropped in. She stayed almost an hour. I didn't begrudge her a minute. Young people are curious, enthusiastic, open. We lose so much of this by the time we're twenty-three. I go to all the meetings of our senior highs. They help keep me curious, enthusiastic, open.

She went downstairs in the morning and died across her ironing board. Twenty-seven years old. Two children. "How do you explain it?" people ask. I want someone to explain it to *me*. Who is going to be a pastor to *me* at such times? I am alone with God and no answers come and then I am expected to go out there and give answers.

An agnostic university student came back to see me. "I tried loving my neighbor," he said, "and all that Christian crap. I tried for three weeks. But it didn't work. It was too boring. Besides, my friends were laughing at me."

Sometimes I think all Christianity takes is a little guts. This boy was working until midnight every night for money to date his girl friend. He worked hard at that. But to stick with Jesus Christ more than three weeks was beyond him.

The books say you should *accept* this kind of person. I don't. I get angry. I barbed the young man for some time. That made *him* angry, and he began to barb me. Just before we stepped into a battle royal, I suggested that if he were really serious about this Christianity business he'd read a book I had for him. Almost as if to spite me, he said he would.

Suddenly I realized how productive my honesty with my own feelings had been, and it made me think there ought to be a study on "The Creative Use of Anger in Counseling."

But now I find out that my student has lost his girl as well as his faith. It makes my anger go. I'm even a little bit angry at myself for being angry.

After a while you may be tempted to tune people out. I have heard it all before. I am post-shock. And I have heard it so many times that sometimes one more time may not get through. Furthermore, I am tempted to think that a little common sense is all that is necessary to clear up many people's problems. Before anyone walks in that door I have to resensitize myself. Maybe that's what prayer is.

Three days ago I was up with them until two o'clock. Today they were in church together. I saw him look up as the communion was passed and swallow hard.

A friend is dead. His heart stopped beating at his desk. His wife called. "Could you come over?" It has saddened me more than anything in my ministry.

Bill is back in jail. He had eaten dinner at our house and played with our children. We talked for five hours. Then he went home and they picked him up.

These things I do not understand tonight. A prostitute who enjoys her work. An addict who enjoys his addiction. A man and a woman who will not come to their daughter's wedding because she is marrying outside her faith.

I have climbed the stairs in this hospital so many times to see so many people. And what have I brought them?

No answer to the man who is leaving his wife. No answer for the alcoholic. No answer for the widow. Will it always be "no answers"? Christ was in the temple asking the rabbis questions. But after the wilderness he had his answers. Why must my wilderness be forty years while his was only forty days?

Because of the "privacy of the confessional" or the "privacy of the pastoral relationship," the minister isn't supposed to share a person's questions with anybody else. Maybe that's what hell is. Being alone with your ultimate questions. The question about death. About adultery. About premarital sex. About dope. About failing grades. The church so often seems bent on perpetuating hell rather than opening heaven.

I have just been with another cancer patient. She is getting worse. But I am better whenever I see her. She has the most radiant faith I think I have ever experienced in these seven years. It is amazing the good that can come from such evil. Like the cross.

The kindergarten class sent me a picture. It was obviously a community effort. It looks like an iceberg with feet. Inside, the teacher wrote, "Thank you for helping God." It was probably in their curriculum to do it, but nevertheless it touched me. If you can begin to think about helping God at the age of five, by the time you're fifty and need *God's* help, it will be there. So many people come into middle age with very little sense of God. I remember an emergency I was called out on the other day. A man was very sick. He never went to church, I was told. "He never got around to it." Everybody's going to need God on that last trip to the hospital, but so few people really think about God before. Then they try to beat death with a God they know nothing about. It can't be done. If these youngsters grow up helping God, they will be ready at any time to be helped by Him.

"Won't you sit here?" And a huge, floppy chair is indicated with a wave of the hand. I am invariably offered the most comfortable chair in the house when I call. The rightful proprietor stands aside, and with a generosity as gracious as it is sometimes self-conscious, he sweeps me onto his throne.

Being offered the chair-of-the-man-of-the-house is baffling to ministers. For one thing, here they are luxuriating in the great man's favorite resting place, while he is perched on an antique. They are embarrassed.

For another thing, the chair prevents their leaving on schedule. In spite of the fact that he has another call to make, the minister cannot suddenly pop up from such plush surroundings and announce that he must be on his way. Furthermore, he may not *want* to pop up. Every fold of the chair entices him to stay with that family the rest of the evening.

Worst yet, the chair-of-the-man-of-the-house is a strong soporific. If the minister is the slightest bit tired, he will soon be responding vaguely and his eyes will be closing for more than a blink. Before he knows it, his head will sag dangerously, and he will have to make a sudden lunge—across the room, say, to pat the dog—in order to keep awake.

When the minister calls he should be offered the kitchen stool. Everyone will come off better.

A baby is born six days after ours. There is no husband. The woman comes to me. She is brought by one of our ex-prisoners. He met her in a bar. Should she put it up for adoption? He called our man who had visited him in jail. The man brought them to me.

Linda is flying home today to die. She had a toothache. They discovered leukemia. She is only twenty-four years old. I can make no sense of it whatever.

It didn't work. There is no argument for God there. They are going to be divorced. God was the only thing that could have saved that marriage. And I was unable to release him.

This is going to be *my* testing. Mrs. Brown has cancer again. It is the fifth time. She is astounding. "I cried a little," she said. "But I'm going to fight it. I'm going to make it." If it had happened to me, I would have gone under.

An hour and a half today to make one call at a hospital. Maybe this is why ministers drive so fast. An insurance man I know says ministers are the best bet in health and longevity, but no company would give them a comparable break in their car insurance. With all the calls that have to be made and shortness of time in which to make them, I can see why. In one three-day period I averaged seventy miles a day.

A woman came to my office in a huff about her marriage. She is, of course, half right. But I won't hear from the other half until I invite him to talk. Four out of five times, in my experience, it is the wife who comes to the pastor first about a shaky marriage. If the husband comes at all, it is usually only after he has been asked. This is understandable if not commendable. The man does not want to admit anything is wrong. Or, if he does admit it, he refuses to believe that he cannot handle it by himself. That's being a *man*. It's also being silly. Marriage is mutual, and whenever one of the partners thinks he can go it alone, look out. I have to look out, too. I get pretty angry at the guy who doesn't try.

I am in a hospital. Anxiety is here. A person never goes to the hospital without thinking dark thoughts. The pastor has his rounds just as the doctor. But he does not feel as adequate. The doctor picks up the chart, chats briefly with the patient, and prescribes. The pastor tries to read the patient's eyes, talks and listens, prays, and leaves. But the anxiety does not always leave with him. The dark thoughts stay. And they stay with the minister, too. He rarely knows the prognosis. And even when the prognosis is known and is bad, the minister is still uneasy. There is no glib answer to death, even if you're a Christian.

One of our boys in college came in to say he's going to be a minister. He is a remarkable young man. When something like this happens it makes you think that all you have gone through has been worthwhile.

The imminent death of this man from cancer is too much for me. He couldn't be more than forty. Several children. Big, strong, nice-looking chap. Again I wish there were somebody to help me bear it. I have told my wife, of course. But the load is so heavy that I feel the need to share it with more people. Maybe that's what the church is. It's a group of people who are willing to distribute the load. "Bear one another's burdens," Paul said, "and so fulfil the law of Christ."

"Nothing personal. They're just not interested." So a church officer described a more-absent-than-present husband and wife. My alternatives in such matters are limited. I can either call this week or next. Christ's call often conflicts with a minister's desires. I have little desire, for instance, to visit these people. If they are made of such soft stuff that they cannot stick with something they have started, that is too bad. If they are so uncreative that they will not suggest ways of relieving their disaffection, I am tempted to say, forget them. Let's let them go, clean the rolls, and spend our time more profitably. But I must stick with them. Like it or not, I have to make that call. In much the same way, I guess, God sticks with me.

I am in my car calling tonight. In this house there is sadness because a grandmother has died. In this one there is hope because a teen-age son is gifted. In this a son left home suddenly. Over here a father is getting established in a new business. Over here a mother has had to go to work. And down the road there, they sometimes talk of divorce. These are real people with real joys and real sorrows. Inexplicably, they open their doors and their hearts to me, a real person with real joys and sorrows, too. And together we open ourselves to the possibility of God.

I went to her house the morning her husband died. There aren't many things you can say. So I let the Word of God say it. I picked up the big old Bible on her table and read the Twenty-third Psalm and John 14 and I Corinthians 13, the love chapter. Then I prayed as best I could. As I turned to leave she said, "Thank you for smiling." But if it had been my wife who had died, there wouldn't have been any smiling. It is so easy to "radiate faith" when it's someone else's hell.

Once I asked a newspaper man why he went to church. Reporters are pretty hard-boiled customers, and whenever you find one who is religious, you've discovered a pretty rare item. "Our little boy was sick once," he explained. "We had to take him to the hospital. Our minister met us there. He stayed several hours." "Well, what did he do?" I asked. "Pray? Read the Bible? Make small talk?" "He was just there," the reporter replied.

A man bowed his head in my office and prayed for our little boy, who is in the hospital. A woman called and said she just wanted to thank me for being here. An elderly lady closed a letter to me with, "We love you." A good deal is made of a minister's pastoral care of his people. But the fact remains that the people do minister to him as well as he to the people. Otherwise he couldn't go on.

A young man I married said he hadn't been in church since the wedding. That was two years ago. This is a direct reflection on my pastoral competence. I had no business marrying this fellow if he was going to take his marriage in a Christian church that lightly. It is also a reflection on his ability to accept a challenge. Christian marriage is a challenge to Christian commitment. Not for him. Nor for his family. They're wonderful people, but they have no relationship to Christ or to a church. They never worship, they never pray, they never say a grace. Consequently my young friend's behavior could have been predicted. No other institution can touch the family as a teacher of religion. If there's no religion in the parents there will rarely be any religion in the children. We're Christians by chromosome as well as conviction. It's just that simple. And just that challenging.

"A lady from the church was just here. She came in a jeep." So I was greeted by a woman recently widowed. Once again my jeep-lady had arrived before me. There's nothing mysterious about my jeep-lady. You find one like her in every church. They are women with big hearts and lots of drive—literally. There is hardly a place my jeep-lady hasn't been. She has called on the old members. She has called on the new ones. She has called on prospective members. And when she has run out of members, she has gone to the nursing homes and the hospitals.

I wish I were as indefatigable. Calling is usually the first priority to slip. There are so many more urgent matters, it seems. This is unfortunate. Calling is one of the best ways for a pastor to keep in touch with people. You see the house and the neighborhood and the children. You hear the transistor radios and the cap guns. You pick up the complaints and the longings. Next time the church talks about raising the pastor's salary, I think I'll ask them for a good, tough, second-hand jeep instead.

I learned that a person had written a minister regarding one of the minister's church members. The next day the minister called, saying he would look into it. "This is most helpful," he said. "I can't be responsible for what I don't know about."

So often people expect a minister to know all about them, right down to their last neurosis. But it is impossible for a minister to know every instance of need in his congregation. He depends on people telling him, on *their* taking the initiative.

The best call is often the one a person makes on his pastor. He is there for a purpose. He knows he needs help in clarifying his thinking. He knows he needs biblical insight into his problem.

The difficulty, of course, lies right there, in a person's getting up initiative enough to make the call. In this case, for instance, the church member did not like his minister for some reason, and so he was staying away from the services. But would he call the minister to talk it over? Would he make an appointment? Would he invite him for lunch? The chances are he expected the minister to call *him,* after his absence from worship had become conspicuous.

Responsibility for pastoral care is mutual. The best care is that in which the church members are as conscientious in their calling on the pastor as he is in his calling on them.

Our family ate dinner with another church family. It doesn't happen as often as you might think. When it does, I am struck with how I would like to go into every home in the church with a tape recorder (or seismograph, as the case may be). You can tell a lot about a family by the way they behave at the dinner table. Hearing themselves would be quite revealing. Think I'll run an ad in our church paper: "Pastor for Hire. Will Sit in on Family Dinner with Tape Recorder and Give Free Report of Findings."

"My new life is truly a joy to get up to each morning." For every disappointment there is an encouragement. This letter was from a reformed alcoholic. The Christian church can learn many things from Alcoholics Anonymous. Chief among them, perhaps, is the ability to confess. Confession is all but gone from Protestant churches. Nine out of ten converts to Roman Catholicism say that what is most meaningful

to them is the confession. So says an Episcopalian minister.
He ought to know. It's his people—among others—who are
converting.

Whenever I make a call unannounced, the wife will invariably apologize for the condition of her house. I used to toss it
off by saying, "Think nothing of it—our house is just the
same." But that didn't speak too well for *my* wife, so I gave
it up. Then I started to say, "Think nothing of it—I grew up
in a family with six children." But that didn't speak well for
my mother, so I gave it up, too. So now, instead of trying to
identify, I just say, "Think nothing of it," and let it go at that.
It has always puzzled me that women should be so defensive
about the condition of their homes, even when they are im-
maculate. Men never notice such things. You could sweep
the sofa under the piano and it wouldn't bother a man. I
often think that if we spent as much time on the eternal as
we do on the external, we'd all be saints. But maybe that's
just man-talk.

I wish everyone could have a chance at this job. If everyone in the congregation could sit in this chair for a week,
we'd have a lot happier congregation. Each person would see
that there were people whose problems were bigger than his,
and in thinking about *their* problems he would get *his* in the
right perspective. This is really what the "priesthood of all
believers" is all about. Every man is a priest to every other

man. We are all ministers to each other. The other night I was leaving one of our small groups when a man said, "Say, could we pray for you?" It brought me closer to them than the two hours of discussion.

Not long after I came here a woman called the church office to cancel her subscription to the denominational magazine. "We never read it," she said, "and it just clutters up the house." I remonstrated, pointing out that it was good journalism and that the editors were doing a first-rate job of relating religion to life. But to no avail. Before she hung up she asked me who I was. I gave her my name. "Who?" she asked. I gave her my name again and added, "the pastor." "Oh," she said. Then, very quickly, "Thank you," and hung up.

I saw a fellow pastor roaring down a boulevard this afternoon. It reminded me again how most ministers drive too fast. It seems to be an occupational hazard—literally. I'll never forget a long trip I took with three pastors. Two of them drove. They averaged eighty. Of course, they had a meeting to get to. It always seems as though there is a meeting or an emergency. The only way to slow ministers down would be to give them large enough salaries so they could hire chauffeurs and do some of their work in the car.

Well, my friend was rocketing down the street when I horned him, and he pulled over. We both got out and talked there by the side of the road. Strictly shop-talk, buildings and budgets. But it was productive. We exchanged some good ideas. Then as we left, going side by side down the one-way street, my friend leaned out of his window and shouted, "Just been to the hospital. You can't beat the challenge of the ministry!" He's right.

2

Preacher

And if the bugle gives an indistinct sound,
who will get ready for battle?

I Corinthians 14:8

One of the proofs of the divinity of our
gospel is the preaching it has survived.

Woodrow Wilson

Some time between two and four o'clock on Saturdays, depending on the difficulty of the problem, I emerge and go to the mailbox and am happy for the first time in the week. Only then am I free. The freedom lasts until after the last service Sunday. Then I am bound again. In Paul's word, I am a "slave." I am chained to the big questions. And only when I have gone into the darkness and come up with a glimmer of an answer am I free.

You wish you could escape this weekly writing after it has gone on month after month. Then one week when you do escape—in this case because someone else is speaking—you are irascible, waspish, impossible to live with. You have worked just as long hours, but you have accomplished nothing. Only when a thing is written have you accomplished something.

A man said to me after a sermon, "You must learn compassion." He's right, of course. The ability to communicate compassion is a rare gift. Many of the so-called "great" preachers don't have it, while some of their humbler colleagues do. It is a matter of manner as much as anything. A preacher may talk about love with beautiful diction and flawless elocution, but if his mien belies his meaning, his talk will be worthless. On the other hand, he may mumble his words and jumble his thoughts, but if love is in his eyes and manner, his talk will convince. This is not to say that nice guys are the best preachers and poets the worst. Nor is it to say that no preparation is better than much. It is only to say that sometimes the mien can get the meaning across even when the meaning is poorly expressed. In truly great preaching, of course, mien and meaning marry.

Holy Week. I can think of nothing more important than working with these enduring themes. A bill, a poem, a philosophy even—they are evanescent compared with what is going on in the Bible. There is no point in devoting your time—except marginally—to anything less.

If I get a week behind in my filing I'm sunk. It takes me an hour to catch up. Every night I shred magazines and newspapers at my stand-up desk. If I don't get these scraps of evidence filed the next morning, I will have a stack three inches thick by the end of the week.

There is a real danger in preaching of losing yourself—not romantically but literally. Maybe you have a thought that does not square with the gospel. Maybe you'd rather turn your thinking to nonbiblical themes. Maybe you'd rather not preach on a subject but know it is important for your people to hear that subject. The tough thing about this profession is that you have to be continually going into areas you may not want to go into at all. You lose your self, all right. Precisely there, perhaps, is where you discover the meaning of "Whoever loses his life for my sake will find it."

I've had an enjoyable time of it. I've met some fine people. We have lived in nice homes in nice neighborhoods on nice incomes. But I have hardly progressed one inch theologically. Despite the three-thousand-word "essays" every week, I am not much closer to God than I ever was.

"You spend a week preparing your sale," a man said, "and I come here to be sold!" Amen, brother! Keep talking. This is the kind of no-nonsense approach ministers like and rarely hear. People are too deferential. My friend was saying that my sermons had better be good or he wasn't about to come to hear them. I'm with him all the way. Christianity will be "bought" only as its "salesmen" make it attractive. If I am not sure of my product, or if I use tired language to advertise it, or if my demeanor is fawning or arrogant or nonchalant, my "customers" will not buy. For me this means an hour in the study for every minute in the pulpit.

I wonder if people realize how tired a preacher gets of hearing himself talk. Every week he must declaim for twenty minutes. In my case it's sixty minutes because we have three services. After a while this can become pretty tiresome. After a few years it can become deadly. It's not just a matter of being fresh every Sunday. That's not the problem. The problem is that there are so many other people who should be heard, too. The solution seems to be to have another speaker once every three months, no matter what the week off does to you. It should be in the budget. Nobody has a corner on the gospel.

"You believe it so much," she said, coming out of church. "It means so much to you." What I say does. Yes, that's true. But there is so much left unsaid. There is so much new country to explore. I must get out there. See what I can find. I open a tiny window on a cluttered vista every week when I should be standing like Balboa by the Pacific.

Went out of town on the train to make a speech. It is important to get away. Total immersion is fine up to a point. But even the President of the United States gets away occasionally. What it does is get you out of the old patterns and give you new images. Imagination is all. I wrote the better part of one sermon on that train and outlined another.

You always preach to faces. Cathedral services are cold and draughty because the people cannot be seen by the minister. When I see old Mrs. Jones out there, it makes a difference. When a woman's arm is through her husband's, when a high school senior is on the edge of his seat, you never forget it. The minister always carries these faces into his study. This sermon is for Joe, this for Mary, this point for Sally and Jim. In a very real sense it is the people who write the sermon.

Here I am preaching Christianity to people who are already Christians. What sense does that make? Sometimes I think it would be a good idea to sweep all the ministers out of America and into Africa, India, and points east. It would give our country a breather and their countries a glimpse of the gospel. On second thought, though, if an African Ubangi had to glimpse the gospel through *me,* he'd probably be diverted instead of converted.

Everyone has his particular talent, to be sure. But a lot of us are second-raters compared to the men who are really out there on the firing line. Like the layman who spoke to a group of ministers awhile back and put us to shame. He is going to Pakistan as an engineer, to a small town up in the mountains, with his family and his God. Of course, he has something to take, some *thing* to take. He can take his drawing board and build dams and bridges.

What could I take? A Bible? They couldn't read it. A sermon? They couldn't understand it. A prayer? They wouldn't believe it. The only bridge I have is Christ, but without the engineer's bridge, the modern miracle, Pakistanis will rarely accept Him. Laymen are often the best preachers. Jesus was a layman. We took down the engineer's address and drove home to our fat churches.

It was a five-point sermon today—unprecedented, and not likely to happen again. I thought it was too much, but when one of the more perceptive worshipers said, "I wish you had given us more time to think," I knew for sure. Five points are too many for a sermon. So are four. Three is tops. Two-

and one-pointers generally stay with people the longest.
There are dangers, of course. One is that the one- or two-
point sermon won't *go* anywhere or *do* anything. It will spin
around and around like a broken record, making the same
point over and over. This is called laboring the point.

Another is that the preacher will set up a negative first
point so that he can smash it to kingdom come with a positive
second. This is called the straw-man sermon.

A final danger is that of charging off in all directions. This
is called losing the point.

But these dangers may be small when compared with the
danger of overwhelming the listener. With a new point made
every four minutes, he becomes breathless. The sermon may
sparkle. The worshiper may be entertained. But he won't
remember the theme.

I feel that I said the same thing today that I have said in
sermons before. The language was different, of course, but
the thought was the same.

I am the victim of two obsessions. One is that I may be
running out of a gospel. There are certain aspects of Christ's
teaching that ignite me. They form my particular emphasis.
But after a few years I realize that I am repeating myself and
may be running out of fire.

The other obsession is that I will never have enough time
to say all that I have to say. The Bible is such flint to my steel
that I seem to be continually on fire.

One obsession should cancel the other. But it never does.

That's why every week of sermon writing is another agony—and ecstasy.

I preached an old sermon this week. It is fatal. There's nothing staler than an old sermon. I've got a cracker barrel as deep as the next fellow's, but I rarely dig into it. Only when I get caught by too much emergency pastoral work.

It's not that the old sermon isn't good. It's often better than the current crop, and certainly better than one done in a few hours. It's just that it's old. It no longer comes alive for me.

But there's still vitality in it, that's the curious thing. It can still speak to people. The congregational memory is very short. Let the sermon lie fallow for two years, and you can always use it again. People won't remember. That's why some preachers get away with murder. They never have to turn out anything new once their barrel is a couple of years deep.

On the other hand, the best preacher I know not only writes many new sermons each year but also revises old ones. And he preaches them over and over, in his own church and all over the country. He is constantly working on them, making what was once good better. First he forged, then he tempered, then he honed.

Well, I went in there honed this week, but I guess I hadn't honed enough. It didn't come off. But several people said they liked it.

To put myself under this yoke when I could be free. To force my thoughts into the biblical mold. To be answerable to God for every one of them. "My conscience is captive to the word of God," Luther said. That's just the problem. I don't like being a convict any more than anyone else.

I may fight it, but it is this having to produce every week that keeps me going. The weekly clutch at integration. "The momentary stay against confusion," Frost said. "This is all I care for," Keats wrote, "all I live for."

A frustrated colleague said, "I no sooner get into my office to work on my sermon than the telephone rings." If it's an emergency, fine, but if it isn't, something is wrong with his priorities. It wasn't. The congregation should know that the minister is in his study all morning, every morning, working on his sermon. It is the only time he has to think and he should have it.

A man came in, and as he put it, "in love," gave me some good criticism. He explained why my recent sermons were missing the mark as far as he and a couple of other people were concerned. This was almost two years ago now, but I have never forgotten it. It took courage on his part, and it was immensely helpful to me. All the time he was talking, though, I had to fight down the urge to leap to a spirited defense. Since then, I have wondered how many other ministers are as fortunate.

Not long ago I heard a very sharp man criticizing his minister for ineffective preaching. "Why don't you talk to him about it?" I asked. "That's not my prerogative," he replied. "If it isn't yours," I pursued, "whose is it?" Ministers need this kind of honesty.

Many ministers let their wives be their critics. And some wives are remarkably adept. But it isn't the same. Wives too often think down the same grooves as their husbands. Others let the old ladies be their critics. This may be good for the ego, but it is bad for the growth. The best method is to take it on the chin occasionally from a man whose judgment you respect.

Easter is next Sunday. The sermon for it is the most difficult one a minister has to preach. It is hard because the idea of the resurrection itself is hard. I am forced to come to grips with the central idea of my religion, and I cannot do it by talking about the pretty spring flowers.

People have heard about the resurrection since their first day in Sunday school, but they have not always believed what they heard. Either the resurrection is the greatest fact or the greatest fraud in the history of mankind, and the congregation must leave on Easter morning decided which. This means a sermon etched in steel.

Also I have to get over a lot of hostility toward the Easter crowd. People will be there who won't be back until Christmas. I have to resist the impulse to let them have it or to leave the pulpit saying I will be back later to preach to any who will be back next week.

A man on the phone said he wanted to come over and punch me in the nose. It was about the first point in the Easter sermon. If a person does not believe that Christ has risen, I said, then he is not a Christian.

"Come ahead," I invited him. But he hasn't. And now it is several weeks since he called.

I'm sorry. I don't particularly want a punch in the nose, but I do want give and take. Preachers are often accused of missing the mark. But they aren't always told where the mark is.

It may be because the average person does not enjoy communicating with his pastor. Perhaps the pastor is so used to talking he doesn't listen well.

When I was in seminary, I remember going up to a famous preacher and asking him for an appointment to discuss the sermon he had just preached. "No," the preacher said, "I never do that. Once they're preached they're preached and that's it."

One experience like that can rebuff a layman for years. So when a man says he wants to punch me in the nose for a sermon, I say, "Come ahead."

I am starting to turn down speaking invitations. I never used to. There seems to be no point in taking the time to do these one-night stands. You never go deep. There is no chance for dialogue. You are rarely invited back. It just doesn't seem worth it. Better to spend the time thinking— or with your family.

It would be nice some day to relax. I haven't had a good conversation in a month. It is the sermons. There is no relaxation until they are done. Every week they pound at you. It is a devilish tough business. But every Saturday morning there is the hope of a miracle.

Something's wrong. I haven't written anything good in five years. Good enough for them, of course, and I get my pay check. But not good enough for me. Two of the smartest men in the congregation congratulated me on the sermon last week. But there was hardly an original thought in it. It was a pastiche. And the style—there was none.

Strange to say, but people like the tough, hard-hitting sermons. Today I laid us all out in lavender. If we are going to be a church, I suggested, we must study the Bible, share our religious experiences, and serve society. Afterward one of the more respected men in the congregation came up and said, "They come to hear this kind of sermon."

It has happened before. Once I described "the emptiness of man" for about twenty minutes. Afterward several people came up and said, "This was your best." Another time I preached on the necessity of social action, pointing out all the negative things that happen when we don't act. "You're going to have that one mimeographed, aren't you?" several people inquired.

Someone told me of a recent poll of Presbyterian women. They were asked which they preferred, soft preaching or hard? Ninety-eight per cent preferred hard. We ran a similar poll with our Board here and got a similar result.

It is interesting that Christ used the hard sermon often. "Do not think that I have come to bring peace on earth," he said. "I have not come to bring peace, but a sword." "You hypocrites! Well did Isaiah prophesy of you, when he said: 'This people honors me with their lips, but their heart is far from me'." "You brood of vipers! How can you speak good, when you are evil?"

Christ never backed away from hard preaching. Maybe that's why he said, "The good news of the kingdom of God is preached, and every one enters it violently."

I came out of the pulpit today and preached a sermon to myself. I tried to give what any man in the congregation would expect of his minister. I guess I did it because people usually think a minister only preaches to them.

Unfortunately, such noninclusive preaching is rife. Why, I'll never know. It thrives on the second person—"You sinners!"—and the imperative mood—"Repent!"—and the stentorian voice. It always preaches *to* people, or *at* them, or *down to* them, or *against* them. It uses hell-fire-and-brimstone, pulpit pounding, finger waving, and all the unfortunate stereotypes of "preaching." It is this sulphurous preaching which people have in mind when they say "Don't preach to me!"

Inclusive preaching, on the other hand, is always careful to include the preacher as one of the sinners. This means "we" and "let us" and talking *with* people as well as to them.

It means conversation rather than oration, inspiration rather than perspiration. I have heard this kind of preaching, and it makes me wish I were a layman so I could hear it more often. It is very difficult to do, and I don't always do it.

Here I am on vacation, sitting in a service in another city. I look forward to services like this. They often mean more to me than conducting my own. But it's going pretty badly this morning. The preacher has been speaking for twenty-five minutes now, and it seems as though that's about the amount of time it took him to prepare. I hope next week he takes more time to think. But I won't be back to find out.

I have preached a few times without a manuscript. But it was not wise. Part of the trick to writing a sermon is to write it. Too many ministers go into the pulpit Sunday morning with a scrap of an outline or, worse yet, with nothing at all. Somewhere they got the idea that they could get up there and preach. It can't be done. To extemporize is to victimize, and the victim is the congregation.

"Write the vision," the Lord told Habakkuk. If I do not write my sermons, I will be all over the lot. I must marble them with the right words in the right places. Otherwise they will lack cut and thrust. So many sermons remind me of number 9 irons—plenty of loft, but not much drive. It takes time, though, to straighten out your thinking. And the minister, God bless him, is probably as lazy as the next fellow.

But that's no excuse. A sloppy sermon wastes everybody's time—including God's.

Two high-school seniors preached the sermon today. They did so well that one woman after hearing them drove home, pulled her teen-age daughter out of bed, and came back— with daughter—to hear them again.

A woman is thinking of leaving the church because she wants "peace" not "challenge." God knows I want it, too. But I want honesty more. Better a tortured integrity than a phony peace. So far she has stayed with us.

Not long ago I spoke with a man widely known for his trenchant sermons. "What is the most important part of your ministry?" I asked him. "Counseling alcoholics and unwed mothers," he replied.

3

Politician

Seek justice.

Isaiah 1:17

I fear the silence of the churches
more than the shouts of the angry multitudes.

Martin Luther King, Jr.

"Aren't you the guy that's running for mayor?"

"Yes, sir, I'm the one."

"Well, you're going to lose by fifty thousand votes," an armchair politician greeted me.

I was running for mayor of Albany, the capital of New York State, a city proud of its tradition, oldest surviving community in the original thirteen states, home of loyal patriots and great statesmen.

It is also a city ruled by the last of the old-style political bosses and as such, down-at-the-heels, cynical, corrupt.

I was up against a machine whose power had been absolute for forty years. I was bucking its tough-minded old boss, "Uncle Dan" O'Connell, an ex-convict whose subjects wage an annual contest with a stop watch in re-electing him Democratic Chairman of Albany County. The latest record time of their formal meeting—forty seconds.

Governors Thomas E. Dewey and Nelson A. Rockefeller, from their Republican capitol fortress a stone's throw from city hall, have tried to bring down this Democratic Goliath, Daniel P. O'Connell. They have not succeeded.

It became my turn to try in 1961.

I was the young idealist, a Protestant minister shocked after two years in Albany by the tales of votes being bought, and voting booths being peered into; by reading in the paper about the ninety-year-old fire chief whose underpaid firemen were discovered looting a jewelry store while one of their buddies was suffocating downstairs in an out-of-date gas mask; by seeing the policemen ignoring the triple-parked cars and stalled traffic and driving through the potholed streets in Buicks.

I spoke out about the obvious political and physical deterioration.

People contacted me, and I listened and learned about the power beneath the surface—about "Uncle Dan's" carrot and stick, the carrots being city jobs, of which Albany has more proportionately than any other city in New York State, and the sticks being property tax manipulations, the surest guarantee of a vote because they ally your politics with your pocketbook; about the annual pre-election "contributions" to the party by the city employees, many of whom work for eighty-five cents an hour; about the 4,500 declared Republicans in a city of 130,000, who had not elected anyone to anything in the memory of a generation, and about the thousands of other Republicans who were registered as Democrats.

A woman called me to tell of the ten-dollar bill slapped down on her mantle before the last election by a Democratic politician. A prominent businessman told me of the Democrat who offered to "fix up" his assessment. A clergyman wrote me about a man who had been stood up against a wall by the police and worked over so thoroughly he couldn't stand.

Then our little party was organized to change things, and its leaders said I was the one to carry the flag.

Well-meaning friends warned, "Look, let's run a middle-aged Catholic businessman who's lived in Albany all his life. You're a Presbyterian minister in a city over 60 per cent Catholic. It'd be folly. Besides, you have a good job here, a fine future with the church, a wife and family. Why jeopardize everything when you know you haven't got a chance?"

Person after person was interviewed. Most said they were with us 100 per cent. But when it came to being the leader of the reform party, the answer again and again was, "I'm awfully sorry, I just can't take the risk."

Others said, "This isn't the way to go about it. You can't beat them at their own game. Political action won't win. You've got to educate the people first. It'll take time before you can get votes."

Such warnings were, of course, well reasoned and sensible. But our group felt it was time to cut the forty years of palaver and get down to action.

We got together one night in my living room. There were a dentist, a lawyer, two labor leaders, two insurance salesmen, a graduate student in political science, a furniture dealer, an executive of a publishing house.

We decided we could not work through the Democrats. "Uncle Dan" was not about to make room for us. Furthermore, a good part of our support would have to come from Republicans. But we could not work through them, either, because we did not want to alienate Democrats and because the Republican party was notoriously ineffective.

So we launched a new party. We called it CURE, the Citizens' United Reform Effort. There was a lot to cure.

Our immediate need was enough signatures to put us on the ballot. Going into a neighborhood to circulate a nominating petition was an experience none of us had had before.

"Oh, no, I couldn't do that," a woman said with a trace of fear when asked for her signature.

"You think I'm crazy? I sign your petition and my taxes go up like that," a man said with a snap of his fingers.

I spent two of the loneliest hours of my life in the ward where Daniel O'Connell grew up. There weren't many signatures. But as I came away from a house, I heard a voice calling to me from the shadows. It was a sixteen-year-old boy.

"My dad didn't sign, did he?" the boy said.

"No," I replied.

"Well, I would if I could, and all my buddies would, too."

Eventually we got twice as many signatures as we needed, and our campaign manager presented me with a ten-cent-store trophy. It was inscribed, "TO THE WORLD'S GREATEST GAMBLER."

The issues came more easily than the signatures.

Albany is in the political textbooks for what is known as the assessment racket. The taxes on a house often go up automatically when a new owner moves in. They come down automatically—that is, without long and costly court action—when he lets the Democratic ward heeler "take care of it," or enrolls Democratic.

A young couple moved into a modest home. The taxes were on an assessed valuation of $3,700. Before long it was discovered that they were Republicans. The assessed valuation was more than tripled, to $12,500.

The assessment racket works the other way, too. A woman signed the petition for our party. Promptly she was visited by the Democratic committeeman in her district.

"What's the matter?" he asked. "Haven't we done enough for you?"

"As a matter of fact, you haven't," she said.

"How would two hundred dollars less on your assessment be?" the politician ventured.

One-party rule also has resulted in tax delinquencies totaling $9 million. In January 1961, it was discovered that three thousand current tax bills had been returned to city hall by the Post Office as undeliverable. They had been addressed to vacant lots, to a corporation fifteen years defunct, and to persons long since dead. Testimony before a state crime-probing commission showed that public officials were not even using telephone directories to try to locate tax evaders.

The nonpartisan State Commission of Investigation also found that the mayor, a Yale honor graduate with one of the great names in American business, was compromising taxes, a role for which he admitted there was no legal basis. It found that Albany's state senator and county clerk had realized whopping sums through real-estate deals involving delinquent properties. The county clerk's activities attracted so much public attention that O'Connell decided it would be better not to run him for re-election.

When I met the clerk on a street corner during the campaign, I asked him why he wasn't running again. He replied that he had accumulated enough in his retirement fund, so he didn't need the job.

A policeman told me that he was given a badge, a pistol, and a night stick, and told he was a policeman. The policemen aren't given ammunition for target practice, he said. But they do ride Buicks. These cars are bought one by one from a local dealer without regard for the law that requires competitive bidding on city purchases of more than a thousand dollars.

Under the one-party rule, restaurant owners have found it wise to vend their cigarettes and music from certain types of machines. Using a different type is likely to bring Health Department inspectors thicker than flies, and at the first plop of grease on the counter the owner may well lose his license.

Recently an owner opened with different machines. The next morning rocks were through his windows. Coincidence?

"Sure, votes have had to be bought," a highly placed politician said in a lecture on religion and politics in the church I served. "The going rate is five dollars. But the bum whose vote we buy for five bucks is no different from the person whose assessment we lower two hundred dollars and who then votes our way."

"We have had to put the peek on people occasionally," he added. Nearly every voter in Albany knows the stories, some documented, some not, about sandpapered curtains and high-wattage light bulbs in the voting booths, and about the Democratic politician who was found belly down on a floor above looking through a knothole into a voting booth.

CURE poll-watchers, fresh from a two-hour course in election law, made certain there would be no vote spying, but the myths persisted.

A fireman called me up to say, "I sure wish I could vote for you."

I assured him we had poll-watchers.

"The Democrats would know how I voted," he insisted, "and then I would lose my job, and my mother would be thrown out of her apartment in the public-housing project."

With issues like these we had a strong platform. It was underwritten by a "Bill of Rights for Albanians" that called for, among other things, "the right to work for and do business with the government without having to pay for the privilege." We were aiming at the alleged 10 per cent kickback expected in return for municipal contracts and at the annual shakedown of city employees. "This is my pay envelope—total, $39," a city foreman wrote me. "Today I must turn this over to hold my job."

Armed with our platform and "Bill of Rights," we went to the factories at six in the morning, driving our 1921 campaign Buick (1921 for the year the Democrats took over, and a Buick to remind the voters that every time they saw a police car they were out of pocket fifteen hundred dollars). I went with a group of mothers who had left their homes before their children were awake. We passed out coffee and donuts and literature. We were thrown out at one factory. At another we drank the coffee ourselves. No one wanted to be seen with the opposition candidate.

We went to the major traffic arteries and stood in the middle of the road, greeting the people on their way to and from work.

We went to the shops and the neighborhoods, stopped at the bars, climbed the fourth-floor walk-ups, attended the coffee klatsches.

I spoke to the men's clubs and the women's groups, at rallies and schools, and on radio and television.

I accepted every invitation to speak. My opponent, Erastus Corning II, who was being run for an unprecedented fifth term, accepted none. I accepted every invitation to debate. Corning accepted none.

The Kiwanis Club rescinded its invitation to me to speak.

The high school civics teacher was told he would have to cancel his. The parochial high school reporters were told they could not print their interview with me. The student editor of the St. Rose College paper was told the same. The editor, a young woman, had sat for hours in the mayor's office trying to get a comparable interview with him. It never was granted. Nor did the mayor answer any of the high-minded questions asked of the candidates by the League of Women Voters.

Soon some of my friends at the church were calling for my resignation. I had taken a leave of absence.

I opened my mail one afternoon to find a letter in red calling me a communist.

I went up to shake hands with two men on a sidewalk and they put their right hands under their left armpits.

I came home to my wife a week after she had given birth to our second child to find she had been told by one of the anonymous telephone callers to get out of town.

This was the campaign.

I lost the election. I received just under 16,000 votes to just over 49,000 for Corning.

But because of our party, Corning received the lowest plurality of his career. And we polled more votes than the Republicans.

Of course, neither of these facts obscured the big fact that I got clobbered. "Uncle Dan" steam-rollered me as everyone said he would. Why, then, did I run?

Because there are some things you believe in and go to bat for, regardless. In America, one of these things is two-party politics. Another is good government. Another is the city in which you live. You want it to be a good place to raise your family.

I ran because I felt it is not just the bad that bad men do but the good that good men do not do that corrupts a community. It is precisely men and women with good jobs and fine futures who should be in politics. Otherwise politics will become dirty by default.

We were to blame for Albany, every last one of us. We had tolerated monopoly in politics that we would never have tolerated in our economy. We had tolerated mediocrity that we would have abhorred in our jobs. We had tolerated temporizing that we would never have stood for in our personal relationships.

Like it or not, I was caught up in a fight for power. I went in there to slug it out for the things I believed. I wanted to see power used for the good of the many rather than for the greed of the few.

Finally, I ran because I was convinced that religion and politics mix. Not in the narrow sense of a Christian political party or a state church, but in the broad sense of morality being more than a one-shot deal on Sunday morning.

If "thou shalt not steal" meant anything, it meant that a bunch of political hacks should get their hands out of the public till.

If "thou shalt not covet" meant anything, it meant that monopolies have no place in your home town.

If "thou shalt not bear false witness" meant anything, it meant that a political party had no business—after all the television shows and newspaper ads and everything else—certifying to the secretary of state, as our opposition did, that campaign income had been "none" and campaign expenses "none."

If "thou shalt love" meant anything, it certainly meant that I had a responsibility to the little children who had to stage a demonstration in the streets to get a playground after one of their playmates was run over and killed by a car.

I ran for these reasons. And I lost. But only by 33,000 votes.

CURE's influence continues. The armchair politician no doubt still prophesies on a side street. But his chair has begun to tip.

Five years later to the night. One o'clock in the morning. Chuck just called. We won. Our man took the congress seat. He carried the county by 141 votes. "They're marching up and down State Street," Chuck said. "We're deliriously happy." So am I.

I have a little group over at the jail. It is called "Check Writers Anonymous." We get together every week for an hour. "It's hard to hang on," a man said. "You bite the nail every morning." My job, I suppose, is to hang on with him. And this is no problem, really. I enjoy my time over there. The frustration is that it is just a drop in the bucket. I often think that our priorities are completely wrong. If two thirds of the world are not Christian, we should be spending two thirds of our time in jails and other places where Christ is not notably present. To be sure, Christ is not always present in churches either. But the fact of the matter is that church people have at least stood up in front of several hundred witnesses and said that they were giving their lives to Christ. Presumably they are not perjurers. But this man hasn't even said that. He sees no reason to. Do we see enough?

"You won't know us," one of the men in jail said, "until you take off that suit and put on these blue jeans." Pastors hear this all the time. "You couldn't possibly understand my problem because you are not an alcoholic." "You don't know what I'm talking about because you didn't have a mother like mine." And so on.

I am not convinced. Christ did not have to be an adulterer to understand adultery. But more to the point is that we are all involved in sin. The difference is of degree, not kind. I may not be in jail, but I am a stranger. I am estranged from myself, others, God. It is not that one man is in jail while another is out. It is that we are all strangers. When we realize this we take the first step toward community—that is, toward overcoming our estrangement. The minister as politician is trying to build community.

We've got a controversy going here, and it cuts my sleeping and eating. It's over our denomination's strong racial stand. Our head man has just been thrown into the clink for participating in a sit-in, and an elder has come in with a resolution to excommunicate him.

Out here in the suburbs you sometimes run into this kind of thing. The only way to keep it in perspective is to remember that the elder belongs to a tiny minority and that Christ was not averse to going to jail, either.

The deeper issue, though, is what it does to my relationship to this elder. I am totally against what he has done. Consequently, I have to watch being totally against him. Because he has done something I do not like, I am tempted not to like him. And it is this that I wrestle with at meals and at night.

Postscript to above. The man left the church. We had lunch, we talked, we enjoyed our time together, and he left the church. I know it's illogical. I know Christ told the disciples to shake the dust off their feet if the gospel was not accepted. But that man's leaving the church gives me as much pain as another man's joining the church gives me joy.

Sometime I am going to have to resolve whether I am going to concentrate on action or ideas. Actually, the good thing about this job is that you can concentrate on both. It won't let you get away with specializing. You become neither a politician on the one hand nor a professor on the other. The preacher is both. It is frustrating, to be sure. But it is less frustrating than all action and no think, or all think and no action.

Cheek-to-jowl on T.V. today with one of the candidates for governor. I was one of a panel asking him gut questions.

Thirty minutes. This is the arena. And the question is whether we are going to win the battle here or in the churches. Are the realists going to win or the idealists? The compromisers or the absolutists? It will have to be both. We need Christian politicians and political Christians. Like Christ. Like the disciples. They carried the battle all the way to the arenas.

This drawing board was a happy discovery. Now I can read three newspapers a day and half a dozen periodicals a week. You keep up with what's going on in your local, national, and world communities, but you don't dawdle. The temptation is to read all of a newspaper or magazine. They are not that important. Stonewall Jackson did all his reading off the mantlepiece. It helps.

There is the temptation to go all the way with the doer and leave the thinker behind. Whenever you do the one to the exclusion of the other you will be in trouble. A politician who doesn't think is as harmful as a preacher who doesn't act. The sin of the one is expedience and the sin of the other irrelevance.

I am in a fight. You don't have to be in politics to be in battles. The elders of the church are opposed to signing the fair-housing ad of the Council of Churches. Never fight a major battle on a minor front, Reinhold Niebuhr once said. It is good advice. This, however, is a major front.

Thunder. I am holding my little girl in my arms. There was terror in her face at one crash. I can only think of the millions of children who have heard the thunder of war and then, in the ultimate terror, been killed. Not one child must be allowed to die. What a grand sentiment. The average Protestant gives five cents a week to foreign missions. He is that excited about world community in the name of Christ.

I am in a quandary. One of the best ways to be effective in a community is to belong to a political party. It is the parties that elect the community leaders. But when it is known that I belong to a party, I automatically become less effective with parishioners in the other party. What I say about social problems is written off as propaganda, motivated by partisan rather than religious fervor. What to do? I could be an independent. But then I have no real say in choosing the nominees. I could declare my allegiance to the majority party in the congregation. But that for a minister is not always honest, since the congregation may be 95 per cent the party he is not. The only answer seems to be to take a stand and let the criticism come. The astounding thing is that, when the relationship between pastor and people is right, the criticism is almost nil.

I am impressed with the way people take hold. We have several task forces—to the jail, the nursing homes, the interracial nursery school. Recently we launched a new one. Two thirds of the youngsters in an elementary school become high school dropouts. Within forty-eight hours we had twenty people who would go. They will read and talk with a child during class. The task forces are all run by young women. Their average age must be twenty-eight.

It's the persistence that counts. Here's a president of a company visiting a boy every week in jail. Here's an accountant who has been over at that jail weekly for three years. Here's a young orthodontist who spent fifty hours with a man. The man gets out and within three weeks he is back in jail. So is the young orthodontist.

If only I had the intelligence to spend more of my time getting people to do these things and less of my time getting them down to the church headquarters to sit around and look profound at committee meetings.

The accountant is also a deacon. He almost never makes the monthly meeting. Why? He is in jail. I may be getting smarter.

A reporter called from the newspaper. I tried to get him to talk with someone else, but he insisted on talking with me. It was embarrassing. I don't like talking about myself or "my" programs. In the first place, the programs are always those of the whole church and not just the minister. And in the second place, such articles often make the minister look as though he is "pushing" himself.

One way out of the dilemma is never to talk to newspapers. But this is not always responsible. There is much going on in churches that is newsworthy. But we rarely read it. This seems anomalous from people who are supposed to be broadcasting "the good news."

Another way out is to talk to the papers regularly. This, however, may assume that more is going on in churches than really is. Furthermore, it opens the church to the charge of publicity-seeking.

Perhaps the best way to share an insight and help create community is to charge a church officer with contacting the paper about specific programs at specific times. In this way the minister is gotten off the hook, the church is presented in the best light, and people are able to read about the exciting new breakthroughs in a church's ministry.

This is perfectly legitimate news. It should not bother the church to see their name in print. Let's get Christians out of the pews and into the news.

I am here in a jail two days before Christmas. One of the boys they are bringing has nobody else in the world. It staggers the imagination that you could have nobody else. That is the way it was for Christ at the end. That's why I came, I guess. There are better ways to spend your time at Christmas than in jail. Are there?

We received a national award of sorts for our interracial nursery school. And we are just human enough to be proud of it. The women who teach, and the ones who baby sit for the ones who teach, log incredible hours. To be sure, "There is no end to the good you can do if you don't care who gets the credit." But an occasional pat-on-the-back like this is helpful. I often think that if *someone* just thanked a church school teacher for teaching, or a nursing home visitor for visiting, or a family for taking in a foreign student, we'd have a lot more teachers, visitors, and motivated families. I try to write such letters occasionally. But all too often I miss. Of course, I am *supposed* to write them. The thank-yous that really count are the ones from other church members.

I met one of our officers at a meeting today. Only we didn't sit together. It was a legislative hearing, and he was on one side of the question while I was on the other. But we chatted amicably before and after.

This is the way it should be. We may disagree on public issues, but if we can do so tolerantly there should never be any trouble. The main thing is that we were both in there speaking on the issues as we saw them.

Some people feel, of course, that the minister has no business saying anything on public matters. But the minister is a citizen just like everyone else, and he has an opinion just like everyone else, and he should be allowed to voice his opinion just like everyone else.

In certain cases the minister's opinion will carry great weight. Whenever a moral question is involved, the minister's opinion is always anticipated and ultimately known— either by his expression of it or by his silence. When ministers say nothing about the evil of ghetto housing in their cities, for instance, their opinion is known: they condone it.

The trouble comes when either form of speaking goes

against the grain of the congregation. But the minister cannot always be reflecting the opinion of his congregation; he must also be molding it. So he speaks his conscience—a good old Protestant principle—and lets the chips fall.

I spoke my conscience at the legislative hearing. My friend spoke his. And there were no chips. There seldom are.

Whenever I am tangling with a hot issue, I console myself by remembering that Christ was often in hot water, too. You don't talk about loving your enemies, going the second mile, turning the other cheek, renouncing all you have, without raising hackles.

There are times in every minister's ministry when he must call a spade a spade. The Word of God cuts like a knife through racial injustice, international distrust, microscopic mission budgets, piddling programs for delinquents and alcoholics, nonexistent programs for parolees, out-of-work fathers, mentally ill out-patients.

It is through the minister, often, that the Word of God strikes. This may not always be pleasant, but it is necessary. "Whatever I command you," God said to Jeremiah, "you shall speak."

"My diocese is said to be on the boil," says the Anglican Bishop of Southwark in England. "If that is so, I accept it as a compliment. Boiling water is better than tepid. It can cleanse and generate power."

The minister never ducks a good controversy. Behold the turtle, it has been said. He makes progress only when he sticks his neck out.

The superintendent of the jail called me. He said he had a man eligible for parole if he could only get him a job. I called one of the men in the church. I painted it very black. Grand larceny, alcoholism, divorced, no roots, no initiative, little hope. "I'll see what I can do," he said. The next week the parolee reported for work.

A theologian has said the church is going to win or lose its battle for existence in the suburbs. I believe it. We had to call a special meeting of the Board to decide whether our church would sign that fair-housing ad. You shouldn't have to call a special meeting for that. It should be as uncontroversial as the Lord's Prayer.

During the meeting, one of the elders said, "I was all set to vote against this when it came up at the last meeting. But then I got to thinking. I remembered how a Jewish couple bought a home down the street from us when I was a kid. Some of the other boys and I pestered them pretty hard. It was a very childish thing to do. Frankly, I think it's time we grew up. I'm voting for this thing."

The motion carried.

We're going to win.

4

Priest

Let us offer to God acceptable worship,
with reverence and awe.

Hebrews 12:28

The important thing is that the individual
goes home from church with zeal
and ambition to fight in the living-room.

Sören Kierkegaard

When I look out over the congregation on Sunday morning, I think several thoughts. First, that I am inadequate. Second, that there are people out there better than I. Third, that nevertheless I am the one to do it.

Anyone who thinks ministers are pompous, or even smug, has either the wrong idea or the wrong minister. Most ministers have as sober a view of themselves as any group of people I know. They honestly feel they are not worthy of leading in worship. They feel as inadequate as Moses did before God at the burning bush.

But they also know that, in spite of all their shortcomings, they have been called by these people to rocket them into the week with God first. And it is with this thought that thousands of ministers around the world are able to go into the services on Sunday morning with their shoulders back.

After the services on Sunday it is a curious mixture of beauty and terror. The beauty is in a job well done and a sense of the rightness of things. Somehow, in spite of yourself, by sheer grace, the Word of God managed to break through. But the terror is in a job incredibly bungled no matter how good, and in a nagging despair no matter how violent the struggle to beat chaos into form. Most days the beauty and terror go together. There is no heaven, apparently, without hell.

What I do up there on Sunday morning may be the only thing the average guy sees done for God all week. Therefore it must be so well done that he will remember it for the next six days. He must go out of there stunned.

The parking lot is filling. The people are filing into the church. Here come a young man, his wife, and baby girl. Here is an attorney. Here an elderly couple. Here a boy and a girl.

I am continually struck by the fact that these people are leaving home, recreation, and Sunday paper to get dressed up on their day off and come here. The power of God is very great.

Of course, there are some who come because the wife or husband wants them to. Others come, I'm told, because it's the thing to do, or they want to be seen. Still others come because they've been going to church all their lives; it was expected of them, and now they expect it of their children, and so on.

What is curious is that the motives of ministers in coming to worship are never examined as carefully. The man up there on Sunday morning is assumed to be good, selfless, humble, dedicated, and all the rest. He may be, of course, but all too often he isn't. Or, put it this way, all too often *I* am not.

I can think of nothing that makes me a better worshiper on Sunday morning than that attorney. I may be, *at the moment,* a better priest because of my training. But that does not make me a better priest. When that lawyer saves a lonely boy from jail, as this one has, he may open a far wider window on God than I with all my courses in liturgics and homiletics.

A visitor commented on "the little things" in the service today. By "little things" she meant the invocation, the introductions to scripture and prayer, and the offering. It is the first time this has ever happened.

Somewhere during the course of the hour, nearly every Protestant service runs the danger of the ad lib. It usually occurs at transitional moments or at those times when the minister cannot refer to notes. The peril is great only because the preparation is nil. A minister thinks he can get away with looking his congregation in the eye and saying whatever wanders into his head. He can't.

Every element of the service must be crafted. Nothing can be left to chance. Some of the banalities offered as "announcements," for instance, are an insult to the Lord and an affront to the congregation. "If you can come to our beef barbecue next Thursday night at half-past six, please be sure to call Mrs. Jones. She can be reached at. . . ."

A service's entire "build" can be smashed by a "little thing." It may be little, but it still requires thought.

I was at the ministers' association this morning. When it came time for the singing, we belted out half a dozen hymns —from pietistic to liberal, to keep everyone happy—and we could have kept going for hours. Ministers love to sing. This does not mean they all have good voices, but it does mean they have enthusiasm, and plenty of it. Two hundred ministers can make as much noise as a congregation of two thousand. Most ministers despair over their congregation's singing ability. They can never understand why the singing is so feeble. The upshot is that each minister is forced to resort to his own larynx. That is why you hear them booming down the aisle on Sunday morning, always fervent, and just a little flat.

Oddly enough, I can remember only three times in the last seven years when people have spoken to me after the service about the prayers. This is strange because the prayers are second only to the sermon in importance. A lot of thought goes into them. I know some ministers who take as much care in writing the prayers as they do in a day's work on the sermon itself. Occasionally I build them around the newspaper, opening it up and reading from it in the pulpit. The prayers tend to be relevant this way. And the crackling keeps people awake.

I don't suppose there is a pastor anywhere who has not had a child whisper in one of his services, "Mommy, is that God speaking?" A mother reported that it happened to me recently, and it set me thinking. Maybe some of us *do* think it is God speaking. If the besetting sin of the laity is laziness, certainly the besetting sin of the clergy is dogmatism. We're always right. We've worked for our position, we've read, we've written, and we've been around. Furthermore, we're paid. So when we step up there on Sunday morning or into the committee meeting or into the home, it's God speaking, all right.

There's a fellow in the church who has said to me on several occasions, "Judge not, that you be not judged." The next time a person tells me he hasn't cracked the Bible in five years, I'm going to remember what this man said. It's good advice to keep that dogmatism leashed.

Sunday is Mother's Day. We were making up the order of service and I asked the secretary the name of the person who had given the flowers. She said it was a fourteen-year-old boy, in honor of his mother.

During the summer we have two services, and this Sunday at both and at the same point in each, a meadow lark sang. It was during the prayers. I was astonished. To have such natural beauty in a service does not happen often. Fortunately, I had the good sense to keep quiet during the second service and let the meadow lark do the praying.

A woman apologized to a church officer for her husband's never being in church. "The yard work keeps him pretty busy," she said. You hear this kind of thing all the time. I've never known why. If a man is a Christian he will want to utilize the major resources for Christian worship at least once a week. Most churches are too big. They carry too many nonworshipers on their roles. I sat next to a fellow at lunch today who didn't even know his minister's name. If a man misses four meetings of his Rotary Club in a year, he's out. If a boy shows up at an Indian Guide meeting without his father, he doesn't get in. If a man doesn't show up for work, he's fired. This kind of no-nonsense approach makes sense in any organization. It ought to make sense in the Christian church. Certainly Christ is as important as crabgrass.

A visitor came out of the service saying it was the finest communion he had ever attended. His reaction is not typical. Communion is so little appreciated in most Protestant churches that they can bring themselves to it only four times a year. Even Episcopalians, who take the sacrament most seriously, find their early communion services sparsely attended. And in England they are hardly attended at all. Communion should be the high point in every Christian's experience. In the communion drama a group of dissident individualists is somehow bound into the beloved community. It's a good theory.

It was six o'clock and my wife had just announced dinner when a church officer called on the telephone. He was trying to put together his meditation for the Board meeting the next night. He was still downtown at his office.

The beans can burn for this kind of thing any day. Here is a man who never before had a vital relationship to God, let alone to a church, trying to get down on paper his new relationship to both.

Exporting the worship from the church to the home isn't easy. So from the pulpit I reminded everyone that I would be happy to go to any home where family worship was difficult. That was nine months ago. There hasn't been an invitation yet.

I wish I were disturbed more often. I get called in on the big things all right—death and divorce, for instance, are always front runners. But somehow people have the idea that for such "little" things as family worship the minister should not be bothered.

The typical Protestant conception of worship is, "Who did you hear this morning?" One way out of this meager understanding of worship is to get the people to do more of the work. After all, the word "liturgy" comes from the Greek meaning "the work of the people."

To be sure, the minister is the ancient priest offering the sacrifice at the altar on behalf of the people. He is also a representative to the people on behalf of God. But he is still very much a man. This means that he is sacrificing *with* the people as well as *for* them.

The closer relationship of minister and people means that they are both involved in the people's work. No longer does the priest do it all. There are long silent prayers, one minute or more. Church officers lead in the prayers. The people say —and sing—"Amen." They participate in responsive readings, unison readings, and collects. They even participate in the sermon by meditating before and after it is preached. Some Sunday I'm going to ask *them* to preach it—twenty minutes of silence punctuated by anyone who wants to speak.

It is most interesting that there is a "liturgical movement" abroad in the churches. Most parish priests would say, "high time."

We went out to dinner tonight and the host asked the blessing. This was unusual on several counts: (1) that there was any blessing at all; (2) that the host asked it; and (3) that he didn't ask me to ask it.

I am always uneasy when I sit down to a meal in someone's home. I want a prayer of thanks to be offered because I think it is helpful to remind ourselves of the God-dimension. But I want the prayer to be offered in the right way.

Ministers can tell at once whether the family usually says grace, or whether they are just saying it that night for his benefit. They can also tell at once who normally leads the grace—father, mother, or children.

The best blessing is always spontaneous. It may be offered by any member of the family, as he or she may request, or as the father, the age-old spiritual leader of the home, may request.

When a minister is present, the worst blessing, as far as he is concerned, is the one which he is requested to ask. It suggests that the family is not sure enough of itself to ask its own.

Almost equally poor is the one the mother has to remind the father to remind everyone at the table to recite.

Most men do not say grace gracefully. It embarrasses them. That's why I was impressed when this man thanked God for our being there and for the food. He proved that there are priests in the home as well as the temple.

I received a fee today for performing a service. This is always embarrassing. There is no such thing as a fee in a church. No member should feel he has to pay his minister extra for wedding, funeral, baptism, counseling. Such services are part of his minister's ministry, and acceptance of remuneration for them only serves to perpetuate an outmoded practice.

On the other hand, should a person wish to express his thanks to God on such an occasion through extra giving, he may either ask the minister to send his contribution to a church charity, or he may send it himself to the church charity of his choice. Ministers always encourage giving, but it should be the right giving at the right time for the right reason. Ministerial fees are like church bazaars. The giving is right but the recipient is wrong. Fortunately, both are on the way out.

It's a beautiful Easter. No clouds, no wind, sun blazing, and 125 per cent attendance. But my joy in quantity is tempered by my cynicism about quality. How can the twice-a-year Christian really be serious about his faith? I suppose if one were to take a poll he would find that what raises the clerical ire more than anything else is the phony Christian. This is the man or woman who belongs to a church but couldn't care less. Why do such people get the clergy's dander up? Because they've taken a stand in support of Jesus Christ, and then they've let Him down. I'll take an honest atheist to a phony Christian any day.

Of course, what goes on in church is often uninspiring. The preacher has a bad day, the service is old and cold, you can get better music on the radio. If this is so, the preacher should know it. He should be told.

On the other hand, what goes on in the parishioner is often uninspiring, too. He had a bad Saturday night, he'd rather be playing golf, he doesn't want to concentrate for an hour on one of his days off. If this is so, the parishioner should know it. He, too, should be told. Before we put the pastor out to pasture, let's get all the people under the steeple.

"We talk about the church at cocktail parties." When one of your members tells you *that,* you know you're in business as a church. I was delighted. All too often we think of the church as that *place* where we *go* on *Sunday*. If the church were ever that localized, either in space or time, it would never have made it out of the first century. Sometimes I wish we would put huge padlocks on the doors of the church buildings after the Sunday service to show people that the church isn't just there, it is out in the world getting its feet dirty.

Ministers are asked to pray all over the place. Everything from a political rally to a convention seems to require the divine blessing.

On the one hand, I would prefer that the praying be done by the people involved. There is something artificial about bringing in the "expert" to do the group's praying for them. The priesthood of all believers suffers.

On the other hand, ministers are realists enough to know that if they decline the invitation to pray the program committee will simply find another clergyman. So when the invitation comes in, the minister treats it seriously. This is an opportunity, he reasons, for potentially creative service.

The average person at such functions regards the invocation as necessary but boring. His eyes are on the dinner or the floor. With a carefully wrought invocation the minister can slice through the boredom and just possibly surprise people with God.

Invocation at a Republican County Convention

O Thou in whom we live and move and have our deepest being, we begin this political meeting by acknowledging our dependence upon thee. We begin by saying that our religion and politics mix.

O Lord, thou art the creator and sustainer of all things, including political things. Thou art the redeemer of all life, including political life. Help us never to forget that thou dost love politicians as well as pastors; that thy Holy Spirit can be in a smoke-filled room as well as in an incense-filled church; and that we can be near thee in a meeting of the local ward club as well as in a meeting of the local parish.

We ask tonight that thou wouldst give us the fortitude to fight the political fight; the courage to stand for what we believe; the magnanimity to compromise; and the wisdom not to fight a major battle on a minor front.

O Lord, help us never to let politics—or religion—become dirty by default. Give us the temerity to become involved; give us the courage to care; the tenacity to lobby; the exuberance to campaign; the endurance to sit through meetings like this.

Help us, Lord, to keep the moral soldered to the political, in the fusion which has made our country great. Help us to roll up our sleeves and get in there and slug it out for the things we believe. Help us to realize that this is the only way to bring our religion out of the abstract into the concrete, and the only way to lift our politics out of the trivial into the meaningful.

Therefore, Lord, we ask tonight that thou wouldst make our love more political and our politics more loving. Help us to love our neighbors, as Jesus said, and to spell that love out in good candidates, good bills, and good laws. Help us also to "seek justice," as Isaiah said, and to spell that justice out in loving poor people, drunks, and bums, as well as church people, pastors, and politicians.

Finally, God, to keep our religion and our politics mixed, help us to remember, at least once in a while, that thou dost love Democrats as well as Republicans. Amen.

The funeral is at two-thirty. They were digging the grave this morning. The silent men. I have seen them so often. And I have seen the families who come to the funerals. Their self-possession is always astonishing. I have seen uncontrollable emotion only once. It was an atheist. Nor have I seen it in nursing homes. An old lady once said to me, "You see the last mile here." But not in her eyes. Nor is uncontrollable emotion in hospitals. Men at the bedsides of women, women at the bedsides of men. It is always the same—the amazing resilience of the human spirit. And it is always the same for me—the knowledge that if it were happening to me, I would not be half so resilient as they. How ironic that I am "the minister" when it is they who minister to me.

A man dropped in one afternoon. "How would you like to pray together one morning every week?" he asked. "Take your time. Think about it." I needed no time. This is the kind of thing ministers dream about. Every Thursday morning now we meet at my study before work. It's a good thing for me as well as for him. Contrary to popular opinion, ministers don't spend a great deal of their time praying. Luther worked an hour every morning at it, but that was four hundred years ago.

A man who has never belonged to a church closed a small group meeting the other night with a prayer he had written:

We here in this group are striving for some very important understandings, God. With your help, we have all been very fortunate—we have earned the important material things in life. But more and more we realize that all these things we possess still leave us vacant. Our group is together now, God, because we are interested in achieving greater emotional maturity, greater wisdom, and above all a greater understanding and feeling of your love. We ask simply, God, that you guide our progress; that you give us patience and humility and fortitude so that we do not falter short of our goal. We ask that thy will be done. Amen.

When an agnostic father can pray like that because of a small group, I'm for getting the worship out of the sanctuary and into the living room.

5

Teacher

The Lord's servant must . . . be . . . an apt teacher.

II Timothy 2:24

The average untutored adult continues at 50 to
expound religion with the same sort of shallowness
he displayed in college bull sessions at 17.

Sylvan Meyer

A woman called and asked point-blank, "What is the purpose of life?" It was one of those questions the minister as teacher always hopes will come but never seems ready to answer.

"To know God," I ventured.

"Do you?" she asked.

"No," I said. "That's why I'm a minister."

We had an adult class ripping along. Then one day it wizened. Finally it died. Let's say it was the time rather than the teacher. Nobody wants to go out regularly on Sunday nights.

Ministers love to teach. There is a vitality and immediacy they do not get in preaching. Here they take as well as give, they are able to deal with important subjects in a tough, cerebral way.

There is the Bible, for instance. It is, or should be, the most important subject of study in any Christian's life. The minister's job is to make people *want* to study it. And many ministers can, brilliantly. They make the Bible writers leap right out of the book.

There is church history, too. Few things are duller than the recitation of dates and facts, but few things are livelier than hearing a minister who can make the past present.

There is theology, the study of God. It scares everybody. But the good teacher makes it intriguing. He brings it out of the stratosphere into the atmosphere for everyone to enjoy.

With all this to teach, a church without a teaching minister is getting shortchanged. I think I'll go out and try to resurrect that class.

There are times, quite a number of them, when I think I shall go back for a doctorate. But there are also times, more of them, when I think I will not. On the one hand, I want to go all the way with the Bible, I want to bury myself in the incredible poetry and prose of those ancient men, many of them unknown. On the other hand, I can get fairly close to them as it is without carving three more years out of my life.

I must take a course at one of these seminaries next term in the Bible. They give them on selected books. Imagine a whole term with Amos or Isaiah or Paul. The Bible is all.

I preached at one of the area colleges today. Whenever I go to a college I'm exhilarated. People are thinking there. They are reaching for breakthroughs. So often in churches people do not think. Church people can be incredibly dull. They do not apply their brains to anything more engaging than how to cook up a fair to pay the light bill. No wonder the church excites so few people. It is high time we turned our churches into colleges.

A stunning conclusion. I must get back to the Bible, live with the Bible, be absorbed by the Bible. It is the only permanence. The stories, the poems, the myths, the images, the reports—they alone will survive. There is, then, for me, no more important job than trying to make sense of the Bible, to make what was written then mean something now.

I'm going to teach tonight. Two hours. Excitement. I could teach all night.

I accepted a lectionary assignment for a sermon over at the seminary. I have never used a lectionary in my life. But when I read the passage from Ezekiel I was transfixed. "Remove the turban, and take off the crown; things shall not remain as they are. . . . A ruin, ruin, ruin I will make it."

It's the Bible as much as anything that keeps me at this. I have never known anything like it. The power of it. I am mesmerized.

Here I am at a women's society. I am supposed to make the address. A woman has now gone on half an hour longer than she should. I wonder why I get myself into these things. I will read them some Hebrew. That will bring them alive.

I rearranged my office today. Brought the Bible books closer to my desk. It is the only thing we have to offer.

Going home with half a dozen books in my briefcase. Staying up till midnight again. There just doesn't seem to be enough time.

I'm out here giving a series of talks. I'm alone now in the house where I'm staying. Absolute stillness except for a mourning dove. Extraordinary opportunity to work. This tremendous need to get things down, get them explained. And yet the final thing is so elusive. You can't get it down. It is maddening. Is it this curious madness that drives a minister every week?

I am consorting with fundamentalists. They have something I lack. Somehow they have an experience of the Man. It is almost Pauline. To be sure, in many cases it is mixed with deep psychological needs. But who doesn't have needs? If a person can have a fulfilled life with Christ—why not? One other thing you can say for fundamentalists. They know their Bible.

I like to talk with the fellows down at the gas station. It keeps me in touch. We talk about valves and rings and bearings, and they explain to me all the bad habits of my eighty-six horses. I wish we could get down to the nuts and bolts of theology more often. Ministers are often terrible mechanics, mistaking plugs for points. And many laymen couldn't care less how the machinery of theology works. What is needed is the opportunity to sit down and come to grips, in a relaxed fashion, with the great affirmations of our faith. This can't normally be done in a sermon. It can't always be done in a lecture. It has to be done also in a small group where you can hang your feet up on somebody's coffee table and talk until midnight.

I started to tell a young atheist that I didn't understand radio waves, either, but I still accepted them. "Don't give me radio waves," he interrupted. "I want God!" Teaching people who are predisposed *not* to believe is hard. For one thing, they won't listen. For another, they would rather argue than discuss. And for another, they usually succeed in getting your dander up.

The best way to deal with such people is to begin where they are. If a minister tries to tell them where they should be, he's sunk. They know, and they don't want anyone telling them. "What kind of God don't you believe in?" is a good place to start. The atheist will find that he shares a lot of common ground with the minister. Then the minister can begin to build, rationally. Does the universe make more sense with God or without Him? Do love, truth, beauty, goodness, your own existence make more sense with God or without Him? Gradually, "proofs" from experience may be sought. The minister directs the atheist to all sorts of worship services, to prayer, to people for whom God *works,* and to the actual experience of living day in and day out *without* God.

The proofs of the brain are never as convincing as the

proofs of the heart. But if a person really wants God he will fight for both.

Every morning I go to my office, and the challenge to make sense out of God grips me by the lapels and smacks me in the face. And we fight there, God and I, the way a man named Jacob fought 3,500 years ago and a man named Jesus, who prayed, Luke says, until "his sweat became like great drops of blood falling down upon the ground." It is an old struggle, but every day in that office it is new.

A five-year-old came up after the service, shook my hand, and said, "I've got a question for you. Who made God?" This kind of thing happens to church school teachers regularly. I sympathize. In a matter of seconds a depth charge can be laid on your entire theology. There is only one way to deal with such questions. You have to be honest. If I don't know, I say so. If I do know, I answer as simply as possible.

We get into a lot of trouble in churches when young people find that Sunday-school answers are not adequate for high-school questions. The answers have been too quick, too pat. Better no answer than a pat one. Religion is anything but pat. And it should be a cardinal rule of church school and home never to teach a child something that he must unlearn later. It might not be a bad idea, too, to tell ministers not to say anything in services that they cannot explain to five-year-olds. I had a rough time of it Sunday morning.

Here I am trapped in a bookstore. I say "trapped" because once a minister gets into a bookstore it's mighty hard to get him out. Ministers gorge on books. They never get enough of them. They have to have all the latest in novels and theology. Since this is hard on the salary, ministers shop all over the country for the cheapest place to buy their books. They also wait with rocklike patience for the bestsellers to come out in paperback. But it's even harder on the brain than it is on the budget. If a minister were to read all he wanted to read as well as all he should read, he'd have to clip along at three thousand words a minute. My back reading now fills a shelf three years long.

A woman wants to talk about God, so every other Wednesday I go to her house from one to two o'clock. She fixes a pot of coffee, and we talk theology. A man called me the other day, said he wanted to kick around some of the big questions, and wondered if I couldn't meet him for lunch. We were just sitting down to dinner a few nights ago when the telephone rang and a father and his son were both on the line wanting me to settle an argument about the first and third Beatitudes. Were they the same?

These are the kinds of questions a minister is in business to get.

Unfortunately, though, I can think of these four people so readily because their kind of question comes so seldom. You wouldn't believe it, but the number of times people call on a minister to discuss religion is small. That's why I said once that I would be available at any hour of any afternoon or any night to discuss any question anyone might have regarding anything to do with religion. Since I said that nearly a year ago, the number of times I have been called could be counted on my fingers.

The senior-high young people were at our house tonight. Afterward several of them stayed to talk. One of the girls took off her shoes and climbed on a chair to reach the top shelf of the bookcase. Such eagerness is winsome. But we lose it so fast. My job, I guess, is to keep people eager, including myself.

There is an enormous temptation in the ministry to coast. For one thing, the minister knows more about his field than any of his congregation. For another, almost any of his other jobs is preferable to the intellectual slogging required of good teaching. That's why you will find plenty of ministers who are crackerjack organizers but terrible theologians.

The same temptation to coast holds for the congregation, of course. They know so little and the field is so big, why bother?

The best way for the minister to keep his brain going and his knowledge growing is to teach. A minister without an adult class is a minister going downhill. And a congregation that doesn't insist on one and then bulge it at the seams is a congregation on its way to religious illiteracy. We would all do well to reach for the top shelf in our bobby socks.

With children clamoring in the background, a housewife telephoned to read me the first page of a new philosophy book. This is the kind of thing that can set a minister up for a week. It renews his faith in the curiosity of the layman. That faith flickers pretty low at times. We had a series of meetings during Lent, for instance, to study with seminary professors the great Christian themes—Incarnation, Atonement, Resurrection. Average attendance was a smashing fourteen. If laymen brought as much curiosity to their religion as they do to their jobs, the church would be revolutionized. When you're working eight, ten, and twelve hours a day, though, this is tough. And when you're a housewife with three young children, it's next to impossible. I was impressed.

6

Planner

All that Solomon had planned to do in the
house of the Lord and in his own house
he successfully accomplished.

II Chronicles 7:11

If the body of Christ is nailed into an institutional
coffin, how shall there be a resurrection?

William Stringfellow

One of my pet projects has been torpedoed by a committee. I am disconsolate. I'm also annoyed. A minister comes to a church loaded with plans. At last, he thinks, this is the church which will be a church. He stays on at the church still loaded with plans, but his expectations are tempered by his cynicism. Finally he leaves the church with his cynicism tempered by his expectations.

It doesn't always work out this way, of course. But it happens frequently enough to be mentioned.

One of the minister's greatest frustrations is his own people. He sees so clearly the path they should take as a church. He knows in his heart that this is the right path—from his study of Scripture, from his prayer, from his seminary, from his other churches, from the leaders of his present church. But either he is inept in communicating the vision or the people are blind. They do not move down that path, or, if they do, it is with agonizing slowness.

Take the area of benevolences, for instance. Every minister knows that his church should be giving away at least as much as it spends on itself. But only a rare minority of churches do.

Or take the Bible. Every minister knows that church members should be involved in disciplined, regular Bible study. But they are not.

Or take mission. Every minister knows his church should be at the jails, the nursing homes, the hospitals. But not all are, by any means.

Plans for concerted action in these and all areas are slow in coming because democracy is slow. It takes time for one man's vision to become another man's commitment. And it takes even more time for that commitment to become a congregation's plan.

Democracy means education, and education means time, and time means patience. Unfortunately, patience is for saints, which few ministers are. That's why they become annoyed.

And that's why congregations sometimes become annoyed with ministers.

I don't suppose my plan is very different from the next fellow's. Another minister may express it differently, but basically it is the same. Going all the way back to the first century, it is that every church member study, share, and serve the gospel which we so blithely profess.

"They devoted themselves to the apostles' *teaching*." A disciple is a learner in the root sense of the word. A discipline is a way of learning. It is impossible to respond to Christ's challenge without learning exactly what he said and exactly what he meant. This requires good, hard, solid work with the mind. The Christian church begins and ends with the Bible, but the Bible cannot be understood unless the Bible is studied.

"They devoted themselves to the apostles' teaching and *fellowship*." The church is perhaps the one social institution in which deep sharing can take place. Where else can people be so honest? Where else can they relate to each other in such depth? "If one member suffers, all suffer together; if one member is honored, all rejoice together." That is the church.

"Even as the Son of man came not to be served but to *serve.*" Every church member is a servant even as Christ was the suffering servant. His major service is job and home, and his minor service is through the church. In it he seeks to fulfill Christ's reminiscence: "I was hungry and you gave me food, I was thirsty and you gave me drink, I was a stranger and you welcomed me, I was naked and you clothed me, I was sick and you visited me, I was in prison and you came to me."

Sometimes I think committee meetings are an invention of the devil. More time seems to be wasted in them than anywhere else. What is needed, of course, is a good chairman. Without him, you're sunk. With him, something can happen.

In my experience there are two types of chairmen. One is the let-'em-have-it type. He lets the committee have it—right between the eyes. They are his committee; he runs the show, and they are convened solely to lend avoirdupois to his already weighty decisions.

The other kind is the let-'em-take-it type. He lets the committee take the ball—all the way. He sits back; everyone throws in his two-cents' worth, and several hours later they come up with their decision, carefully amended. Most chairmen are of this type.

What is needed is a chairman midway between these extremes. Give me a man with an eye for the clock, an ear for the committee, and an agenda written in concrete, and I will go to his meeting.

I have spent the whole day administrating, and I am not particularly happy at the end of it. It is not that administration is unimportant. It is that you can administrate forever and never be caught up. There is always another person you could be behind to get something done. Occasionally there is someone else ahead of you trying to get something done, and you could catch up.

This is the one place where ministers go haywire most often. Their days begin and end with the telephone. They race from one committee meeting to another. What should be last becomes first, as they ad-minister their congregations instead of ministering to them.

The trouble is that many people, laymen and clergy alike, have gotten it into their heads that for a church to be good it has to have program leaping out the windows and plant to the tune of a quarter of a million dollars. Consequently churches are overorganized and undergalvanized. They are overcommitteed and undercommitted.

The minister becomes nothing more than an executive secretary. He is an organizational gear-greaser. In other words, he is not what he was called to be: pastor, preacher, politician, priest, teacher *first* and *then* ad-minis-trator, or planner.

We do a newsletter every week called "The Challenge." It keeps the people in touch with the plans and the pastor. Often it brings a phone call. It is this keeping in touch that keeps a church moving. Whenever communication breaks down the church breaks down. Churches "split down the middle" are churches in which "people are not speaking to each other." Precisely.

I once knew a minister who spoke of the church as a "spiritual laboratory." It is a convincing metaphor. For one thing, it is scientific, and science these days is usually convincing. For another thing, it suggests experimentation, and experimentation is always exciting. Take belief in God. It is exciting to make an experiment of it. God is the hypothesis, life is the attempt to prove God, the church is the catalyst helping a person make that proof.

Take love. That we should love each other is the Christian hypothesis. Every Christian's life should be the attempt to prove love. The church should be the catalyst helping, encouraging, sometimes goading a person to make that proof.

Take fulfillment. "Whoever loses his life for my sake will find it." That is the Christian hypothesis. Our lives should be an attempt to prove it. Our churches should be the catalysts challenging us to make the proof.

If more people viewed the church as a laboratory for doing basic research into the life of the spirit, there would be more people in churches. It would be too exciting for them to stay away.

Sometimes I think we ought to change the name on our big sign out there from "Church" to "Laboratory," a center for basic and applied religious research.

We have a job here that needs doing. It's one man's job, and I am not the man. Ministers are often expected to do too much. From fixing the boiler to chauffeuring the youth group, they are the ones on tap. After all, the argument goes, they're getting paid, aren't they? But the minister is not hired to do what anyone else can do as well. He is hired *only* to do what others *cannot* do as well. He is hired for his six specialties. In this, the sixth, he does not do everything, but he sees that everything gets done.

A minister told me his church was refurbishing. He said a firm came in with an exorbitant estimate. He told them to do their homework better and come back with a proposal that made sense.

Some people think ministers are so heavenly minded they are of no earthly use. Actually, most ministers have a pretty highly developed practical sense.

Every week they deal with important matters of business. There is the budget, for instance. There are the buildings and grounds. There is the church office. There is the mortgage. In many cases there are the architect and contractor. In all cases there is the relationship of other members of the staff to the plans of the church, be it one janitor or six other ministers.

Because the minister works with the church every day, he is usually far more conversant with its institutional aspects than anyone else. Because he meets with most of the committees, he is usually the only one who has all their monetary needs and program plans in his head. And because he works *at* the church every day, he probably knows what he's talking about when the talk is about refurbishing.

This is heartening to the congregation. They like to think that a man accused of having his head in the clouds also has his feet on the ground.

A colleague was introduced to another colleague, and they found they had a mutual friend. Whereupon the one said to the other, "He's the fellow that always gives me a guilty conscience. I no sooner get a letter off to him than I get one back, and I'm behind in the correspondence again."

Firing back an answer seems to be the only way a minister can keep up with his mail. If he lets it go, within a week it will be deeper than the compost in the church garden.

Keeping up means snatching a few minutes every day. Fortunately our church has a dictating machine, and a secretary to go with it, so my snatching is a snap. Without it, the answering would often be drudgery, and the letters would pile up fast.

Of course, there's one type of mail that never requires any time—the anonymous letter. Currently I am receiving a spate of anti-Semitic and anti-Roman Catholic junk. And there is the vitriol that always comes in when a minister is involved in a community controversy. It is quickly consigned to the wastebasket. If it isn't worth signing, it isn't worth reading.

As to answering the rest of the mail at once, it may be a quirk, but it's a quirk that works.

I have a hard time knowing how we're doing. There are no charts I can put up on the wall to shout our progress. There are no quotas to tell us we're doing well.

We took in a hundred new members last year, but this doesn't mean we're a front-rank church. It mostly means we're in a growing community. We probably should have taken in two hundred.

We raised our budget nearly 50 per cent. But this doesn't prove very much. Most of us are still giving away far less than 10 per cent of our incomes.

We gave away more than we ever had before. This is some indicator, all right. But we're still far from giving away as much as we spend on ourselves.

We averaged 60 per cent of our members in church over all Sundays. This may be well above the national average, but where are the other 40 per cent?

Actually, the best indicators of progress are the ones nobody talks about—the man who visits at the jail now; the woman who came back to her husband; the young person who began to visit at the nursing home. These are the gains, and there are scores more like them.

I broke my watch the other day playing football with the neighborhood children. But I got the thing fixed before it did me much good. Ministers, of all people, seem to be tyrannized by time. A minister's datebook is as crowded as the insides of his watch. There never seems to be enough time into which to pack his days.

This makes for two reactions. One is to give up. Here there is little pretense at keeping a schedule. Many ministers are notorious for being habitually late. The other reaction is to take time by the throat. Every hour of the day is rigidly planned, and the plan is kept, right down to the coffee cup.

I favor the second approach, but there is actually room for both. The first man should learn how to fire more action into his day. And the second should learn how to relax. There is always *some* time during the week when we should leave the watch on the football field.

I talked with a minister yesterday who told me that he spent his entire afternoon picking up the pieces of a job that had never been done. Two high-school girls were supposedly enrolled for a conference by their youth leader. They arrived at the conference and found that they had no beds. Not only did the minister have to enroll them, he even had to get in his car and take them a number of items they had never been told to bring.

Volunteers can be the despair of ministers.

They can also be the joy. We have a man who writes all the checks and keeps all the books. It is a huge job, but he never complains. His wife orders, files, and reports on all the books in the library. Another woman has given countless hours to resettling a refugee family. A man showed me painstaking charts he had made for his Sunday school class. Another man came in with a detailed plan for restructuring the budget. Many others give prodigiously of their time.

The church is a curious mixture of inertia and zeal. A minister is, too.

A woman wrote me a letter saying she wanted to resign from the church. Things had not been going well in her family, and she felt she did not deserve to stay with us. This is like the argument of those outside the church who say they couldn't possibly be in because they're not good enough. Nothing could be farther from the mark. People don't join the church because they're good but because they're bad. The church is a real sinner center. The only difference between the sinners on the inside and those on the outside is that the insiders are trying to do something about their sin. They're more ambitious. They have a plan. The woman stayed.

A man called me for an appointment, and when he came in he told me he was considering joining another church. It wasn't anything against ours. It was just that he had been with us for four years now and he wanted to get another emphasis.

On the one hand, this is the height of responsibility. Many people will just stop going to a church, and then six months later a request will come for their letter of transfer. Never a word of explanation.

On the other hand, this indicates an incomplete understanding of the church. A church is not that *place* where you *go* to get an *emphasis* on *Sunday*. It is the beloved community. And once a person joins it he is a member of the family of Christ. Responsible people do not break up families. If a family is off the mark, they try to reform it from within. They do not run away.

7

Person

Take heed to yourself.

I Timothy 4:16

What is the reality, the essential
person behind all its camouflage?

Paul Tournier

A letter came from a church member.

You there in your cloth of ordainment with all your open doors to men's souls—you walk about their lives and look at will.

We give you our sins and sorrows, our pains and joys. We spread them out, timidly at first, one by one. Then after a time we pour all out.

And you give in return—pardon from Him, consolation from the Scriptures, sympathy from your own compassion, answers to our questions. You give strength to your church, leadership to your followers, aid of your experience to the layman, encouragement to push us ahead.

And we thank you so much.

But when will we see *you?*

Are you afraid to stand too close to your flock? Must you remain without blemish as a father to his son? Have you no sins or sorrows? No joys just bursting? Are you all listening, no sharing? All finished product, no rough raw material?

Who told you to keep your line so straight, your cloak so tight around you? Are you afraid that your treasures, no matter what their shape or color, will be nothing of value to others?

I wonder how many friends a pastor has. It's the image people have of us. We are supposed to be wizards and saints. We are, of course, neither. I do not have all the answers, nor do I lead a better life than the next person. I have, then, two choices—either to coddle the image or be honest. It is no choice, of course. I must be honest. I must give my people at least that. Better an honest sinner than a counterfeit saint. Better to be disliked in honesty than liked in deceit. So when people say, "You wouldn't understand because you're a minister," I tell them I have sinned, too. And when they ask, "Why did my father die?" I tell them I don't know, but I will look for an answer with them.

A woman came in and said, "I hope you dare to be a Daniel." Then she told me about the "lion's den" that "got rid" of my predecessor. And then she went on to the "lion's den" that was forming against me. What could be more typical of churches? It is so juvenile. My reaction used to be, too. But now after a number of years in the game, I just get quietly angry for a few minutes and then forget it.

We walked to the swamp and my five-year-old boy found a hole in a thicket and we crawled through and he found a log and we sat on it and there we watched the trees and a dog and listened to the birds. It is the first time I had done anything alone with my children in as long as I can remember.

I respect Jack highly. He has been my good friend for some time. And today he said over the telephone that

there is no need to try to communicate. I've thought it all out. You can't communicate it. Even when you have found something. Even when you have *been* found by something. All that is needful is to make enough money to assure the security of your wife and children. That's all.

I guess I record this because the temptation to say, "That's all," is as real for me as it is for him. There is this almost daily fight between hope and despair. But for some reason— and it is the reason that keeps me going—I would rather *try* to communicate *something* than give up and communicate nothing. You have to try. Otherwise there is no point in getting out of bed in the morning. What mystifies me is that I know Jack wants to try, too. He is a poet.

August. Vacation. On a mountain. Not until I have climbed the mountain can I pause for the flower.

Home from vacation. Half-past ten at night. A man drops by to say, "I've missed you. It's nice to have you back." That doesn't happen very often. There is an isolation to this job most people don't know about.

A western meadowlark is staking out my office. I can work through cars and telephones and typewriters. But I cannot work through one bird singing.

Cold days. Many fires. I lie in front of them with my children and we tell stories about what we see.

I try to take a day off. Long ago I promised myself—and my wife—I would. But, try as I will, I cannot. The only rest I have is in work. When I am away from my work I am like fingernails across a blackboard.

The best minister to the minister is his wife. She knows him and she loves him. Therefore she can criticize him and support him. Ministers' wives are often excellent critics. But they are even better cheerleaders. Whatever they are, they are a rare species.

Other people minister to the minister. His own children, for instance, keep him in touch with humility and patience. His congregation keep him in touch with himself—in ministering to them he is fulfilling many of his own needs. And other ministers minister to him. Generally a minister will have at least one colleague to whom he can tell anything.

At the youth group banquet I was presented the first award. Two pink ribbons were attached to a circle of white paper. The inscription read: "Least Positive Influence."

The conversation was flowing freely in the barbershop today when it came my turn in the chair. As I stepped in, the barber said, "Hello, Reverend." Instantly the conversation stopped. As a matter of fact, there was precious little talking at all after that.

This was both helpful and not. On the one hand, it served to remind the men of the more genteel forms of expression. But it also served to emphasize my distance from them.

I never wear a clerical collar for this reason. It blares distance. Or, as one of my colleagues put it, "I never want to look at a man over a whitewashed fence."

Next time I go to the barbershop I'll improve the talk by my conversation rather than my appellation. Let's tear those fences down.

"I just wanted to drop by to tell you it's great having you here." A man who stops in on his way home to tell you that is one of the timbers of the forest.

It's not that ministers hear only the worst. Nor is it that ministers are never complimented. It's that out-of-the-way compliments, unlike perfunctory compliments, are rare. And any man who will go out of his way to compliment—not flatter—another man is tall timber.

Ministers get a lot of the wrong kind of praise. They are told their sermons are "wonderful," when they are execrable. They are told their voices are "beautiful," when they are strident. They are praised as "good men," when they feel like crooks.

It is very easy for the clerical head to be turned. Ministers possibly get more daily flattery than any other profession. Everyone knows the puffed-up preacher. He is insufferable.

Consequently, when the right kind of praise is given him, the minister is touched.

I am tired and I am only thirty-two. I want to take a room somewhere and lie down. A day would do it. The images would come back. And the people. Just a little time to reflect on all that has been happening the last three months. In me and to me. Just a little time.

The only trouble with this job is that you're expected to like everybody. It can't be done. Ministers have people they don't like, just like everyone else.

But there is a difference. I may not like a man, but I must go out of my way to try to like him. I must repress my natural reaction in favor of a Christian reaction. If I dislike a man, I am not free to go on disliking him. I have to call him up and invite him out to lunch.

This is what makes the ministry so difficult and yet so invigorating. It is difficult because I don't want to give a free meal to a bum. And it is invigorating because I have to do what I don't want to do.

Of course, going out of your way to try to like a person should be normal for every Christian, not just ministers. But it isn't. The same sense of obligation is not always felt. And right there is the difference. Ministers have a vulcanized sense of duty. "If anyone is going to try to lead the Christian life," they say, "I should be the one."

So, whether I like it or not, I have to make a phone call. Who knows, I may end up liking the guy.

A man told me the other day that his minister was nice enough but not very effective. This may be true, but it would be much more helpful if he told the minister. Ministers are people, and legitimate criticism is always helpful.

So often, however, constructive criticism is considered taboo in churches. People wouldn't dream of suggesting to the minister where he was weak or how he could improve. The only way he can find out is to ask one or two trusted friends, and they are sometimes too close to him to be helpful.

On the other hand, destructive criticism usually gets to him pretty fast. He hears of vigilantes climbing on telephones to protest something he has done. Letters come in. His friends tell him that "people are talking." Others urge him to "go slow."

If he is going to function successfully, the minister must forget his detractors. The minute he begins to bear a grudge —no matter how just—his effectiveness is diminished. A minister is out to prove that love is invincible. To do so, he needs a bad memory for bad criticism.

But he also needs a good memory for good criticism. He must be so mature that he can accept legitimate suggestions without flinching.

"You know," she said, "why we go in early?"

I assumed it was because their family wanted to meditate before the service began.

"We're praying for you."

The complete impossibility of going to sleep. It has been sixteen hours today without stopping. But now there are five books piled in the chair beside my bed and I want to read them all right through the night. I'll have to settle, of course, for just a few more pages. But once again I declare war on sleep. I have it down now to seven hours. But I have never been able to get it down to six.

It strikes me that what a person thinks of a minister, and what the minister *thinks* the person thinks of him, may be two very different things. For instance, a minister may be tempted to buy a sports car. But then he thinks people will think it's too flashy, and he doesn't. Actually, they probably couldn't care less.

Or a minister's wife may decorate their house tastefully. It makes him think people think he's avaricious. Actually, they probably don't give it a second thought.

Or a minister may take a day off. It makes him think people think he should be tending the flock. Actually, they would probably fuss if he didn't take a day off.

It may well be that people are not as conscious of a minister's behavior as he is self-conscious about it. The simplest antidote is for the minister to do what he is always counseling other people to do: Be himself.

I suppose we all are regular victims of "grass-is-greener" thoughts. Maybe a minister is especially. If he is supposed to be reasonably competent in six areas, he may be tempted from time to time to chuck the five and go for the one. There is an enormous temptation in this job to be superficial, to touch lightly—albeit regularly—on each of the six areas and come to grips with none. So the minister quits and goes back to the seminary or to teaching or to becoming a social worker or life insurance salesman or even a pastor on a large staff, specializing in one of the areas. This is not to say that such jobs do not have their own demands. Certainly they, too, call for competence in several different areas. It is only to say that when a minister gives up the ministry he is giving up the broad competence demanded by that particular profession. The six areas have become too broad for him.

Whenever I think my "grass-is-greener" thoughts, however, I invariably seem to boomerang back. It must be the breadth. Or maybe it is that I can think of no other job that offers such breadth *and* depth at once. You have to be reasonably good in these six areas, all right, or you don't survive.

The grass may also be greener, of course, in other places with the *same* job. A minister may be tempted not only to leave his profession but also to "get another church."

The disease sets in normally after three to five years. The minister has things pretty well under control. The machinery is humming. People are joining the church. The budget is inching up. The mortgage is inching down. He knows all the members. The leaders are thinking along the same lines as he.

The Methodists solve the problem by yanking the minister out and firing him into another parish. Other denominations —and churches—often wish they could solve the problem as tidily.

The problem for the minister, however, is whether he has the imagination to go deep as well as wide. Once he has reached out and gotten the six areas "under control," will he bear down in each of them? Once the diver reaches the coral shelf, will he go deeper, or will he go off to another reef?

"I lost my bet," said the head of personnel for one of our corporations. "I bet my wife you'd be gone in two years." But why? Why do people always think ministers are out for the "bigger church"? Why are more money and more members considered moves "up"? We've got the wrong calipers. You don't measure church success the way you do business success. My job is to release God, and I work as hard in a church of six hundred as I would in a church of six thousand with ten ministers. Ministers move down, not up. More accurately, they move up by moving down.

A man was discussing his church and said to me, "I don't like a minister who smokes or drinks. Do you?" Actually, I had never thought about it much. I have minister friends who do neither, and I have minister friends who do both.

What I do think about, now that he mentions it, is why *ministers* should be expected not to smoke or drink. This man has many friends, no doubt, who do both, but he would never say that he disliked them because they did. When he assesses their characters, the fact that they do either probably never enters his head. So why does it when he assesses his minister?

Most ministers plead for equal treatment. Let's knock the minister off his pedestal, they say. Let's crack his goldfish bowl. Let's tear out the last shreds of asceticism. Then we will begin to treat each other as persons rather than images, and we can talk.

When I talk about smoking and drinking, I say that to do either in excess is foolish. Only a fool would willfully damage his body. But to do either in moderation can be one of the amenities of life. The great Swiss theologian, Karl Barth, puffs his pipe and enjoys his glass of beer. Certainly Martin Luther drank. We know Christ drank wine.

The important thing is not a man's simple pleasures, but the depth of his mind and the sensitivity of his heart. And that goes for everyone, including ministers.

It seems to me only fair that if ministers are to be treated as people, certainly people should be treated as ministers.

In a very real sense, the minister's job is to make ministers of laymen. Every man can speak out for Jesus Christ in his community. Every man has people to care for in the name of Christ. Every man can have prayer in his own home. Every man can teach his children about God. Every man can serve in and through a church.

"Every member a minister" might well become a church's motto. I am not the minister of this church. I am only one of its ministers. The day the church is left to the clergy is the day the church begins to die.

If these six jobs are important in my life, there is no reason why they should not be important in every Christian's life. That is what the priesthood of all believers is all about. Every Christian is a minister. My job is to remind him.

The caliber of person you often get in this profession never ceases to amaze me. Take a college friend of mine, for instance. He was president of his class *throughout* high school. He was president of his class *throughout* college. He was awarded the university's highest undergraduate award. And where is he now, with such a brilliant political future? He is serving the church of Christ in a Chicago slum.

Or take the vice-president of our college class—and this was no denominational school, either, but the Ivy League. He is serving the church of Christ in the race-torn South.

Or take the number one liberal arts graduate in that same class. Where did he go the next year? Not to law school or business school or graduate school, but to seminary.

Or take the high-school valedictorian who graduated second in his class from our university and then went on to be first again at the best seminary in the country.

Or the Phi Beta Kappa football player from a rival college who won a Fulbright Fellowship to England. He is now a minister widely known for his writing on renewal in the church.

I am often impressed by how unimpressive I am. When I think how the cause of Christ in one small corner of the globe depends upon me, I am shocked. Anyone but me is my instinctive response.

Ministers have a whopping inferiority complex. They honestly feel they are not good enough for the job. If you ask them their faults, they can discuss them for minutes on end. If you ask them their virtues, they fall silent. Sensitive and critical, it would be hard to fool a minister about himself —which is a good thing, considering all the praise and flattery he gets.

Nevertheless, the minister realizes that the job is his, and he does his best to fill it. Rather than be paralyzed by his faults, he acknowledges them and pushes ahead in spite of them. Fortunately, the job makes the man in the ministry even more than the man makes the job. Weaknesses can often be forged into strengths.

But it is this realization of their weaknesses that helps keep ministers effective. In looking deep down, they have seen their original sin.

I would like to have help on my sermons some weeks, but if you can't do them alone, you can't do them. I would like to have someone to pray with today, but if you haven't the courage to meet God alone, you have lost the fight for faith. I would like to talk over a counseling problem with my friends, but there are some things you can't share without the consent of the people involved.

There is an aloneness to the ministry that may seem romantic but is actually dangerous. It can so easily become loneliness. Loneliness is giving up to aloneness, being beaten by it.

The aloneness of the ministry can become the loneliness of despair. The minister may despair of ever being a first-rate counselor. He may despair of ever being able to produce muscular sermons. He may despair of his inability to have an original relationship with God.

In order to ease the despair, he may turn to various forms of escape. Instead of concentrating more on his counseling, he becomes a first-rate administrator. Instead of hewing out his sermons, he repeats old reliables or filches someone else's. Instead of driving himself to look for a door in the wall, he gives up praying altogether, and reads the prayers from a book at the Sunday service.

Aloneness can produce toughness or despair. The desperate minister is one of the loneliest of men. The tough minister is alone, but he is not lonely. He knows that God is somehow standing by him in his aloneness.

You do one of these things that ministers do, and then it is over and there is an almost uncanny calm. You almost feel guilty about the calm. But it is there.

A man had just died and we were all in a neighbor's home around the table, and I said that I had nothing to say but that the word of God did. And it was very quiet as I read. The telephone rang and the hostess took it off the hook. Down the street some men were working. Everything was muffled by the snow. And when the reading was over we joined hands around the table, the widow and the children and the grandchildren and the neighbors and the girl friend of the grandson, and I said thank you for this man and for the gift of life and for love.

And now, an hour later in this study, with the weekly conflict strewn across my desk, there is this mysterious calm. Maybe God is in retrospect.

It would be helpful if you could have a burning bush, like Moses, or a Damascus Road, like Paul. But it has never worked that way for me. And I know no minister for whom it has worked that way. Most people think ministers have seen a vision or heard a call. But most ministers are as blind and deaf as everyone else. The only difference between them and the next fellow—if there is one at all—is that they are ready day and night to be surprised by God. This is not to say that the light shines and the voice speaks any more for ministers than for anyone else. It is only to say that ministers are on twenty-four-hour alert. Presumably.

I think of the coffin on rollers and the freshly dug dirt and the six little chairs. I think of the young woman with laughter tumulting from her lips as she talks with her husband-to-be. I think of the little boy in an oxygen tent with his teddy bear at the foot of the bed. I think of the mother smiling the smile of first mothers as she tells of the birth of her child.

And then I think of myself and my being there, and of God's coming somehow out of the nowhere into the now, here and being there, too.

Of this gospel I was made a minister
according to the gift of God's grace
which was given me by the working of his power.

Ephesians 3:7